For Tom,
Love ya-
Corrine

FIREPOWER

FIREPOWER

BRUCE QUARRIE

CHARTWELL
BOOKS, INC.

A QUINTET BOOK

Published by Chartwell Books
A Division of Book Sales, Inc.
110 Enterprise Avenue
Secaucus, New Jersey 07094

ISBN 1-55521-294-8

This book was designed and produced by
Quintet Publishing Limited
6 Blundell Street
London N7 9BH

Design Director: Peter Bridgewater
Art Director: Ian Hunt
Designer: Stuart Walden
Editor: Shaun Barrington

Typeset in Great Britain by
Central Southern Typesetters, Eastbourne
Manufactured in Hong Kong by
Regent Publishing Services Limited
Printed in Hong Kong by
South Sea International Press Ltd.,

PICTURE CREDITS

All illustrations for this publication were supplied through Military Archive & Research Services.

t = top; c = centre; b = bottom; l = left; r = right.

Aerospatiale, France: p67; Alvis UK/MARS: p108; Boeing Military Aircraft: p32t; AB Bofors, Sweden: p103; British Aerospace: p57t, 70, 71, 80, 93b, 94, 95, 107b, 116; Bundesheer: p111; Avions M Dassault-Breguet Aviation: p57b, 84–85, 90; Department of Defense, Washington DC/MARS: p14, 16–17, 18l&t, 20–21, 28–29, 32c&b, 33, 34, 36t, 46–47, 76–77, 78, 82, 84t, 91, 96t, 98b, 106, 107t, 121, 122, 123, 124, 125tr; ECPA/MARS: p25, 39t; Euromissile SA: p118; Fairchild Industries: p96b, 97t; Fincatieri: p57c; FMC Corp: p110b; General Dynamics Corp: p15, 27, 42–43, 64; Goodyear Aerospace: p45; Grumman Corp: p83; Howardseewerke GmbH: p47; Imperial War Museum: p9; Ingalls Shipbuilding Corp: p62, 63b; Krauss Maffei GmbH: p105b; Krupp GmbH: p105t; Lockheed Corp: p21, 22b; LTV Aerospace & Defense Co: p120; Marine Nationale, France: p56; MBB GmbH: p74–75; McDonnell Douglas Corp: p30–31, 44, 97b, 98t; Military Archive & Research Services (MARS): p6, 7, 8, 54, 104, 110t; Ministry of Defence/B Quarrie: p39b; Ministry of Defence/MARS: p19, 22t, 38, 40, 41, 46, 48, 50, 54, 58, 60, 65, 115, 117; T Moore/MARS: p102; Naval Photographic Center, Washington DC: p100t; K Niska/MARS: p87, 88; Panavia GmbH: p72–3, 75b; Plessey Radar Ltd: p51; RAF Museum: p12–13; Rheinmetall GmbH: p112–113; Rockwell International: p35; Royal Norwegian Air Force: p88–89; Saab-Scania AB: p81; Salamander Books Ltd: p63t, 76b, 89, 99; SIRPA/MARS: p24–25; Swedish Air Force: p36b; Thyssen, Henschel GmbH: p109; US Air Force/MARS: p13, 37, 79, 84b, 86, 92, 93t, 125tl, c&b; US Army/MARS: p118–119; US Navy/MARS: p16, 23, 26, 30, 42, 52, 53, 59, 61, 68, 100b; Vought Corp: p113, 114–115; Westland Helicopters Ltd: p10–11, 66.

CONTENTS

INTRODUCTION

Firepower is defined by the dictionary as the ability of guns and other weaponry to inflict destruction. In this book we shall look at the ability of modern weapon systems to do just that, on land, at sea, in the air and in space.

Today's weapons are the most devastating the world has ever known, and some cynics would say that the principal measure of man's progress is his ability to destroy. Certainly it is true to say that the nuclear powers – the US, Russia, Britain, China, France, India, Israel and South Africa – have the ability between them to eradicate life on Earth. Fortunately, the policies of deterrence and mutually assured destruction (MAD) have not resulted in a global nuclear war, though the delicate balance has only just been preserved.

In 1973 Egypt and Syria attacked Israel and for a few tense days it looked as though the invasion might succeed. American surveillance satellites detected Israeli preparations to launch Jericho missiles carrying nuclear warheads against their aggressors as a last-ditch measure, a fact confirmed by an SR-71 Blackbird spyplane overflight. In an astonishing display of international cooperation, President Nixon got on the hot line to Premier Brezhnev and a shipment of nuclear warheads was promptly despatched to Egypt for fitting to Soviet-supplied SS-1 Scud missiles. Fortunately, the Israelis succeeded in stabilizing the situation and eventually turned the tables, so their Jerichos were stood down and the Russian transport vessel was able to return to port.

GUNPOWDER AND CANNON

In ancient times firepower relied on human muscle power alone. Then mechanical aids – sling, bow and crossbow, catapult and trebuchet – extended man's reach. The Chinese were the first to discover the power of chemical-energy weapons and used gunpowder in military rockets of dubious accuracy or efficacy for centuries before the secret was first discovered in Europe by Friar Roger Bacon around AD1250. Even then it was nearly a century before the first primitive gun was constructed by the Augustinian monk Berthold Schwarz in Germany, and the earliest surviving picture of such a weapon is in an illustrated manuscript dated 1326.

The first guns were heavy and cumbersome

cast-iron tubes, plugged at one end and banded with iron hoops to help prevent them exploding in the faces of their users. Later bronze was used, being lighter, and over the centuries guns became more mobile, being mounted on wheeled carriages, and later given limbers so that they could be towed more easily by horses or oxen. All these early cannon and the hand-held guns which appeared during the Middle Ages were of smoothbore construction – that is, the inside of the barrel, or bore, was smooth.

Then, in about 1520, a German armourer called August Kotter discovered that if spin could be imparted to a cannonball both the accuracy and the range of a gun were significantly improved. Thus was born the technique known as rifling, in which soft metal bands formed a spiral for a few inches inside the mouth of the barrel. However, these early guns were muzzle-loaders, the explosive charge of gunpowder being poured into the barrel first, then wadded tightly before the cannon or musket ball was pushed down on top of it. The rifling therefore made it more difficult to push the ball down the barrel, so the penalty for the increased range and accuracy was a reduced rate of fire.

The next major advance did not occur until the 19th century: in 1855 W. G. Armstrong invented the breech, which allowed the projectiles to be inserted from the rear of the barrel. This meant the rifling could be extended all the way down the barrel from muzzle to chamber, and eliminated the

ABOVE Berthold Schwarz experimenting with gunpowder in Friburg.

BELOW Crossbows and early muskets, a German illustration dating from around 1430.

LEFT The American M109 gun/howitzer has a calibre of 155mm (6¹⁄₁₀in) and a muzzle velocity of 684m/sec (2,245ft/sec), which gives it a range of 18km (11 miles).

MONS REGONIS.

Johan scradanis inuenior.
Phls Galle fecit

ABOVE By the 16th century artillery had become relatively mobile, but was still principally used during sieges rather than in open battle.

laborious muzzle-loading procedure. By this time the method of rifling itself had also changed, helical grooves being machined into the bore and driving bands fitted to the rear of the projectile, itself no longer a sphere but elongated into the familiar shell shape we know today. Ironically, in recent years the smooth bore has made a comeback, for reasons we shall see.

PROJECTILES

While guns themselves were being progressively developed, so were the projectiles fired from them. One early innovation was the hollow metal sphere packed with gunpowder with a fuze cut to length so that it would explode within the ranks of the enemy. This could not be judged with any accuracy, though, and it was quite common for the fuze to go out in flight; on other occasions the shell would land with the fuze still burning so an alert soldier could pull it out or kick the shell into a puddle to extinguish it. Then came the impact fuze, in which a detonator containing a small quantity of mercury fulminate was inserted into the nose of the shell. This substance explodes on impact with a solid surface, thus detonating the surrounding gunpowder.

Gunpowder itself began to be replaced during the 19th century by other forms of explosive. It was found that cellulose dissolved in nitric acid produced a cotton-like substance which was stable under normal storage conditions (unlike nitroglycerine, which is highly unstable and unsuitable for use in a gun) but would explode upon a hard impact. Cellulose nitrate, more popularly known as guncotton, produced a far greater blast than gunpowder and rapidly supplanted the latter both as a filling for shells and as a propellant.

Later still came the even more powerful trinitrotoluene, or TNT, and trinitrophenol, or lyddite, which were used extensively during the Boer War and World War I. Subsequently, even more powerful explosives have been discovered, among them tetryl, nitropenta and most recently hexogen, which is commonly known as either cyclonite or RDX. Meanwhile, lead azide has replaced mercury fulminate as the initiator or detonator.

WARHEADS

Shells, hand grenades, mines and missile warheads of the pure high-explosive (HE) variety rely on the combined effects of blast and the flying metal fragments of the shell casing to achieve their effect. High-explosive anti-personnel (HEAP) shells are packed with small steel balls as well as explosive to add to the fragmentation effect. There are also forms of high-explosive anti-tank (HEAT) shells.

The earliest anti-tank rounds, developed during World War I, were solid slugs of hardened steel; later tungsten carbide, which is far more dense, replaced steel, and solid tungsten shot is still widely used in tank and anti-tank ammunition although recently shell cores of depleted uranium have also come into existence. The reason for using these denser metals is to give a projectile of given size greater mass, for armour penetration is the product of half a shell's mass and the square of its velocity: in other words, the heavier a projectile is and the the faster it is travelling, the greater will be its armour-piercing ability.

HEAT ROUNDS

That equation only holds good for solid armour-piercing shot. With HEAT rounds velocity – usually measured as muzzle velocity, or the speed at which a shell leaves the gun barrel – is unimportant. It can even be zero in the case of a magnetic mine which is simply slapped against the side of a tank by an infantryman. The HEAT round contains high explosive packed around a hollow cone-shaped plug, either of plastic or metal, blunt end foremost. Over this goes what is known as a ballistic cap – in other words, a streamlined nose. When the tip of the projectile makes contact with a solid object, the explosive charge is detonated and is focused forward as a concentrated stream of plasma which literally burns a hole through that object.

Since a HEAT round does not depend for its effect on the high muzzle velocity imparted by a long rifled barrel, but instead upon the diameter of the cone, it can be fired from smoothbore guns, hence their resurgence. They are also cheaper to manufacture – which is probably a major reason for their popularity in the Soviet Union – and simpler to service, and the barrels last longer. HEAT rounds do

not spin (indeed, the spin imparted by a rifled barrel would actually work to their disadvantage, since centrifugal force would dissipate the effect of the explosive charge), so they are fitted with fins which open out when they leave the barrel to prevent them tumbling. Without the fins they would be grossly inaccurate, just like cannonballs from early artillery pieces.

ABOVE A British 18-pounder field gun in action at Arras in 1917.

APFSDS ROUNDS

HEAT rounds are capable under test conditions of penetrating a far greater thickness of armour plate than a solid-cored round, but the further from the vertical their angle of incidence to the target, the more their effect is dispersed – and modern tanks have frontal armour plate at least 30° from the vertical. The same is true of solid shot, but in recent years British armourers have pioneered a new type of ammunition designated APFSDS (armour-piercing, fin-stabilized, discarding sabot).

Armour-piercing discarding sabot rounds date back to World War II and involve a projectile enclosed in the front of a case of greater diameter: the sabot. Being bigger than the projectile, the sabot fits into a barrel of greater diameter, or 'larger calibre' in artillery terms. After the complete missile leaves the gun barrel the sabot falls away, and the energy from the relatively enormous propellant charge is concentrated in the projectile, accelerating it to a much higher velocity than a full-calibre shell.

The British development is to fit the sabot with plastic driving rings to fit a rifled barrel, and once the sabot is discarded fins take over the task of keeping the projectile on a flat and accurate course. This means that HEAT warheads can be fired from rifled barrels with no diminution of their effectiveness, and to greater ranges and at higher accuracies than can be achieved with a smoothbore weapon.

HESH ROUNDS

Another type of armour-piercing round, no longer widely used, is the high-explosive squash head (HESH), whose plastic explosive charge spreads itself flat on the armour plate of a tank before exploding. It does not actually penetrate the armour plate of a tank before exploding. Instead the detonation of the warhead is designed to create a strong shock wave that knocks a scab of plate off the inside of the tank; the scab then ricochets around slicing through equipment and bodies with equal impartiality.

One reason why HESH rounds have fallen into disuse is because they need to be far larger and heavier than solid AP or HEAT equivalents: another is that they are totally ineffectual against Chobham armour. So called because it was developed by the British Fighting Vehicle Research and Development Establishment (FVRDE) at Chobham, in Surrey, Chobham armour is still secret, but it is known to be made of a combination of materials, including ceramics and plastics, and can defeat most anti-tank weapons.

A gun's calibre is the inside diameter of its barrel, and is today almost universally ex-

ABOVE A Westland Lynx helicopter fires a salvo of 81mm (3⅕ in) air-to-ground rockets.

as well as land, sea and airborne weapons for use against aircraft. Ships' guns are essentially similar to land-based weapons, being rifled breech-loaders, although during World Wars I and II they were often larger than most land-based guns because water is so efficient at absorbing recoil forces. Where they differ is in fire control equipment rather than actual construction, for a ship's gunnery officer has to contend not only with the fact that his own and an enemy vessel are both moving, so the angle and range are constantly shifting, but also with the fact that both vessels are probably rolling and pitching as well. Today a mixture of sophisticated over-the-horizon radar systems, computerized guidance and automatic loaders make naval gunnery very accurate indeed.

Similar systems, although using laser sighting rather than radar ranging, are employed in the latest generation of tanks, and the small but powerful onboard microcomputer takes into account not just the movement of the vehicle and the target over the ground but also air temperature, wind strength and direction, barrel temperature and even barrel wear. With such modern systems, virtually every shot is guaranteed to be a hit.

Although missiles have largely supplanted guns on modern warships, most classes retain some form of main gun armament, usually of 100-150mm (4-6in) calibre. These are principally retained for use against shore targets in support of an amphibious operation, as in the Falklands, for example. Indeed, the need for naval gunnery support of land operations became so critical during the war in Vietnam that the US Navy had some of its old World War II battleships brought out of mothballs, and has subsequently refurbished them, their original 16in guns now being supplemented by Tomahawk cruise missiles and other systems.

ANTI-AIRCRAFT GUNS

Some of the greatest strides in recent decades have been in the field of anti-aircraft (AA) gunnery. The first anti-aircraft guns were simply existing artillery pieces mounted on modified carriages to enable them to fire at greater elevations. Then came the pressure fuze, which was sensitive to atmospheric density and could be preset to detonate at a specific altitude.

The pressure fuze was followed during World War II by the proximity fuze: this con-

pressed in millimetres, although there are a few surviving guns with calibres given in inches. The length of a gun barrel is, traditionally, always expressed as a number of calibres rather than in feet or metres, so a 50mm L/60 gun would have a calibre of 50mm and a barrel length of 60 times that – 3,000mm or 3m. Generally speaking, the longer a gun's barrel, the greater is its muzzle velocity, because the expanding gas from the propellant charge has more time in which to impart energy to the projectile. And an increase in muzzle velocity translates into an extension of range.

MOVING TARGETS

Of course, artillery is not just used against tanks and personnel: there are also shipboard systems for use against ships and shore targets,

11

tained a small radio transceiver which emitted a continuous beam of radio energy which was reflected back by a solid metallic object such as an aircraft; when the return signal was strong enough, indicating the target was close, the shell exploded.

The proximity fuze made AA fire much more accurate, though bigger targets reflected stronger return signals, so a shell would explode further away from a four-engined bomber than from a single-engined fighter, for example. Since fighters were smaller, faster and more manoeuvrable targets in any case, enormous numbers of anti-aircraft rounds had to be pumped into the air to achieve a hit: even then most aircraft could sustain considerable damage and still remain airworthy. Even so, far more aircraft were brought down by AA fire from the ground or from ships than were ever destroyed in air-to-air combat during World War II. The same was true in Vietnam, though there the principal weapons were surface-to-air missiles (SAMs).

GUIDED MISSILES

The greatest advances in post-war weaponry have been in the fields of missiles and their guidance systems. It was ironic that, because the Treaty of Versailles which ended World War I prohibited Germany from developing any new artillery pieces, the Germans turned their attention to rockets, which were not mentioned in the treaty. By the end of World War II, as a result, the Germans had made greater strides in rocketry than any other nation. As is well known, German scientists made enormous contributions to the postwar American and Soviet space and missile programmes, while the V1 flying bomb led ultimately to today's cruise missiles.

Less well known are the smaller German tactical missiles, which included the supersonic Wasserfall radio-guided SAM and the Ruhrstahl X-4 wire-guided missile. The latter laid the foundations for many modern ground- and helicopter-launched anti-tank systems, since a wire-guided projectile is invulnerable to jamming by electronic countermeasures (ECM). The Germans also pioneered missiles that homed on their targets' own infra-red (heat) emissions, as well as radar and television guidance, all of which techniques are widely used in modern systems. Similar guidance

systems have been applied to 'smart' bombs and artillery projectiles.

An enormous amount of effort is expended on anti-radiation missiles, usually aircraft-launched, which home on an enemy's air surveillance and anti-aircraft guidance radars. The only way the radar operators can avoid such missiles is by shutting down their equipment, so the missiles can achieve their objective, even if temporarily, whether they hit the target or not. And in the fast-moving battlefield environment, putting a radar out of action even for a few seconds can enable an aircraft to penetrate the defences and reach its real target.

ANTI-SUBMARINE WEAPONS

Another recent development in the missile field has been the anti-submarine missile which delivers a torpedo or depth charge to the vicinity of a hostile submarine. The depth charges can have nuclear warheads and are capable of destroying all known submarines, though determining the target's position is an enormously difficult task despite arrays of sensors on the seabed, satellite observation and the use of maritime patrol aircraft equipped with delicate detection equipment. Such airborne systems, include sonobuoys, which float near the suspected location of a submarine and radio their information back to the aircraft circling overhead; magnetic anomaly detection (MAD) gear, which senses the minute variations in the Earth's magnetic field caused by the passage of a large submerged metallic object; and infrared sensors which can pick up the faint traces of colder water displaced to the surface by the passing of a submerged submarine.

When we talk of modern firepower, then, we are really talking about immensely complicated electronic and visual systems, large teams of people, and, inevitably, sophisticated computers and complex communications to bring the weapons themselves to bear. In this book we shall look at complete weapons systems and see how all the elements are brought together, beginning with the most potent of all – the nuclear missile.

ABOVE The German V1 was the precursor of today's cruise missiles. The 'doodlebugs' are seen crossing the English coast in this wartime painting by F. Salisbury.

RIGHT A trio of Tomahawk air-launched cruise missiles beneath the wing of a Rockwell B-1B strategic bomber.

1

THE NUCLEAR ARENA

Despite the euphoria surrounding the December 1987 agreement between President Ronald Reagan and Premier Gorbachov on intermediate-range nuclear arms reduction, it must not be forgotten that the weapons to be dismantled over the next three years represent only the tip of a massive iceberg. The missiles concerned are the American ground-launched Tomahawk cruise missile (256 of which are based in Europe), the US Army's Pershing II (108 of which are based in West Germany), and the Soviet SS-4, SS-12/22, SS-20 and SS-23; the total number of Russian missiles involved is 690. These figures represent only about four per cent of the world's total nuclear arsenal, but the agreement is at least a step in the right direction.

BGM-109 TOMAHAWK

The controversial Tomahawk, so detested by the peace campaigners because it is essentially a first-strike weapon, is the US Air Force's version of the BGM-109 series of missiles developed since 1972 for the US Navy. The missiles are carried in sealed containers mounted on special transporter/erector/ launcher (TEL) vehicles; once fueled and deployed they can be left unattended for months at a time.

Tomahawk is launched to its cruise speed of 885km/h (550mph) by a 3,175kg (7,000lb) thrust solid-fuel rocket, after which its Williams turbofan engine takes over. The missile has a range of 2,500km (1,550 miles) and its inertial guidance system is coupled to a digital computer and a radar altimeter which constantly scans the ground ahead; the computer compares the profile of the ground below it with information in its data storage banks to ensure it is on course. This facility gives the cruise missile a terrain-following ability and allows it to use hills and other obstacles to hide it from enemy radars and other sensors – a necessary precaution since, being subsonic, it is vulnerable to conventional anti-aircraft fire.

The exact size of Tomahawk's nuclear warhead is officially classified but is generally acknowledged to be in the 200kT (kilotonne) range. A kilotonne is equivalent to a thousand tonnes of TNT and a megatonne to a million tonnes; to put these figures into perspective, the German V2 rocket had a one-tonne warhead of conventional high explosive while the atomic bombs which devastated Hiroshima

and Nagasaki in August 1945 were each of 20kT. One Tomahawk, therefore, can deliver with far greater accuracy the equivalent of 100 Hiroshima bombs or 2,000 V2s.

PERSHING II

Accuracy of delivery rather than warhead size is the primary consideration when dealing with nuclear weapons. The US Army's Pershing II has a warhead of a mere 15kT compared with the original Pershing I's 400kT, because Pershing II is accurate to within 35-40m (38-44yd) over a distance which can be varied from 160 to 740km (100-460 miles) and also because it penetrates deeply into the ground before exploding. Consequently, hardened underground missile silos, communications centres and

ABOVE BGM-109G Tomahawk cruise missile transporter/ erector/launcher vehicle in the foreground with the missile's launch control centre truck in front.

LEFT The command centre in the NORAD headquarters deep beneath Cheyenne Mountain is built to withstand direct hits from megaton range ICBMs.

RIGHT Launch of a Pershing II 15kT tactical nuclear missile from its own TEL vehicle.

ABOVE USS *Ohio* undergoing sea trials in 1981. While most American submarines have their diving planes mounted on the sail, as here, there is an increasing trend to place them on the hull instead to facilitate operations under the Arctic ice.

headquarters bunkers which could withstand a near miss or an overhead airburst from a much larger warhead would be pulverized by Pershing II.

Pershing II is a two-stage missile powered by a solid-fuel rocket which gives it a terminal velocity of Mach 8+. Flight time to its target is therefore very short, which is one reason why Soviet military planners were so worried by the weapon's deployment in West Germany. They know, as do their opposite numbers in NATO (the North Atlantic Treaty Organization), that the West would have to respond with tactical nuclear missiles within hours of a conventional Soviet assault in Europe. Without this resort, Soviet armoured forces could reach the Channel coast within five days, so greatly do they outnumber their Western equivalents.

SS-12 AND SS-22

Of the Soviet missiles being removed as a result of the treaty, the 112 SS-4s are of an elderly design and were already being phased out. The SS-12, like its more accurate successor, SS-22, is directly comparable to Pershing, except that its 1MT warhead really places it in the strategic rather than the battlefield category. It is carried in a special air-conditioned container on a MAZ-543 TEL vehicle, and its range is estimated to be some 900km (560 miles).

The SS-20 is a more advanced design and is again really a strategic weapon since it has an estimated range of 5,000km (3,100 miles). Moreover, instead of a single warhead, it

contains three 150kT MIRVs (multiple independently-targeted re-entry vehicles) which are said to be accurate to within 750m (820yd). The 440 SS-20s targeted against Europe and China have long been a bone of contention at disarmament talks and their removal following the Reagan/Gorbachov agreement is probably the most significant part of the entire treaty. Virtually nothing is known about the SS-23 except that it is a fairly small and highly mobile truck-mounted missile, and that only 20 are in service.

SUBMARINE-LAUNCHED BALLISTIC MISSILES (SLBMs)

The ballistic-missile submarine is the most potent weapon in the armouries of East and West, not because their missiles are more powerful than land-based ICBMs but because the launch vessels themselves are such elusive targets, being able to remain submerged at great depths for months at a time. The latest and most powerful designs are the American Ohio and Soviet Typhoon classes.

BELOW LEFT Soviet SS-12 Scaleboard missile on its TEL vehicle. Soviet commercial lorries are designed to the same wheelbase as their tactical missile launchers, allowing them to seek out suitable deployment and launch sites in Western Europe while on ostensibly innocent journeys. So far only Norway has taken steps to prevent this practice.

OPPOSITE BELOW An artist's impression of SS-20 missiles in their firing tubes ready to be launched. The removal of these weapons will bring a sigh of relief from NATO planners.

OPPOSITE ABOVE Artist's impression of the TEL vehicle for the SS-23, a hi-tech weapons system which would have posed a grave threat had it not been scrubbed under the Reagan/Gorbachov agreement while only small numbers were operational.

OHIO AND TRIDENT

The name ship of the Ohio class entered service in 1982 and an initial eight vessels are planned to supplement and eventually replace the Lafayette class. The latter are second-generation nuclear ballistic-missile submarines (SSBNs), each armed with 16 Poseidon SLBMs, while the much more sophisticated Ohios carry no fewer than 24 Trident missiles. In addition, each is equipped with four 533mm (21in) torpedo tubes for self-defence. Crew complement is 133 officers and men.

The Trident I (C-4) missile has already been fitted in 12 Lafayette class boats, and will be the principal armament of the four British Van-guard class SSBNs which will replace the Royal Navy's ageing Resolution class Polaris submarines in the mid-1990s. Trident is a three-stage solid-fueled missile with a range of 7,100km (4,400 miles), and carries eight 100kT MIRVs which will in due course be replaced by a new generation of manoeuvrable re-entry vehicles (MaRVs) capable of evading anti-missile defences.

TYPHOON AND SS-N-20

The Soviet Union's Typhoon class submarines, the first of which entered service in 1980, are similar in length to the Ohios but considerably broader; their submerged displacement is a monstrous 29,500 tonnes (29,000 tons) and

RIGHT The rocket engine of a Trident 1 (C-4) bursts into life as it leaps from the surface during a practice launch.

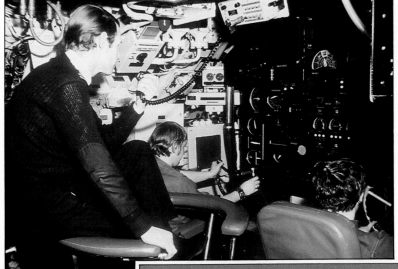

LEFT The control room inside a British Resolution class SSBN with the officer of the watch supervising the planesmen. These vessels are due to be replaced by Trident-armed Vanguard class boats.

RIGHT Launch of a Poseidon missile from an American Lafayette class nuclear submarine.

ABOVE 'Sherwood Forest' – the Poseidon missile compartment in the Lafayette class nuclear submarine USS *John Adams*.

they carry a crew of 150. They are powered by twin shafts, each driven by its own nuclear reactor, and have a submerged speed of 44km/h (24 knots). In addition to their main armament of twenty SS-N-20 SLBMs, they have six 533mm (21in) torpedo tubes for self-defence.

An unusual feature of the Typhoon class is that the missiles are carried forward of the sail, which is situated toward the rear of the vessel. Like all Soviet submarines, the Typhoons are double-hulled: whereas the US Navy abandoned double hull for its nuclear-powered submarines in the interests of a smaller profile, higher speed and quieter running, the Soviets have persevered because of the greater surviv-

ability it provides in a collision or in a combat environment.

Soviet design practice has frequently been criticized by Western naval observers because Soviet submarines are undoubtedly noisier, and therefore easier to detect, than their NATO equivalents, but a disturbing report from the US Naval Institute in October 1987 revealed that the latest Soviet submarines are actually ahead of their American counterparts in several important respects. The report, by the naval architect John J. Engelhardt, cites hull materials and design, maximum diving depth and speed, automation systems and post-attack survivability as areas of Soviet superiority. American

LEFT The French Navy's *Le Redoutable* cruising at speed on the surface. Something not always appreciated about modern submarines is that they can achieve higher speeds submerged than surfaced.

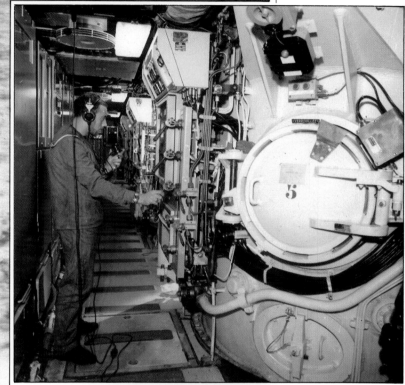

ABOVE The M-20 missile launch room in a French Le Redoutable class SSBN.

submarines, he says, are more manoeuvrable, quieter and have better sound detection equipment (passive sonar) and communications, while their crews are better trained. As for weapon systems, the report says that America and Russia have approximate parity.

OTHER SOVIET AND WESTERN SLBMs

The Soviet SS-N-20 missile in the Typhoon class is a two-stage solid-fueled rocket with a range of 8,300km (5,160 miles) and the ability to carry between six and nine MIRVs of unknown warhead yield. Other Soviet SLBMs include the obsolescent SS-N-5, three of which are carried by the equally obsolescent Hotel II class boats; the liquid-fueled twin-MIRV SS-N-6, 16 of which are carried by Yankee I class submarines; the liquid-fueled SS-N-8, carried by the Hotel III (six missiles), Delta I (12) and Delta II (16) classes, which has a range of 9,100km (5,650 miles) and carries a single 1-2MT warhead; the solid-fueled 1MT SS-N-17, 12 of which are carried by Yankee II class boats; and the liquid-fueled SS-N-18, which has a range of 6,500km (4,040 miles) and three 200kT MIRVs, 16 of which are carried by the Delta III class boats.

Against this array the West has but four types of SLBM, including Trident. The Poseidon missile carried by the US Lafayette class (16 missiles per boat) is a second-generation solid-fueled SLBM with a range of beween 4,000km (2,485 miles) and 5,200km (3,230 miles) depending on warhead, which can vary between 10 and 14 50kT MIRVs. The Polaris, 16 of which are carried by each of Britain's four Resolution class submarines, is now decidedly obsolescent and in urgent need of replacement by Trident. The missile has been in service since 1967, and despite being modernized under the Chevaline programme it lacks the range and accuracy of Trident; range is given as 4,600km (2,860 miles) but warhead size is classified. Finally, the six French Le Redoutable class nuclear submarines each carry 16 home-grown MSBS M-20 missiles: currently being replaced by the M-4, this three-stage solid-fueled SLBM has a range of 4,000km (2,485 miles) and carries six 150kT MIRVs.

No details are available of the CSS-NX-3 SLBMs carried by the new Chinese Xia class nuclear submarines, though each of the six vessels under construction houses 16 missiles.

ABOVE USS *Boston,* a Los Angeles class SSN, on patrol in the Atlantic.

RIGHT Dramatic view of the Los Angeles class attack submarine USS *Birmingham* crash-surfacing during trials.

ABOVE A US Navy BGM-109 cruise missile after launch.

SUBMARINE-LAUNCHED CRUISE MISSILES (SLCMs)

In recent years the subsonic air-breathing cruise-missile has come into its own, not least because it can be stored for months without servicing, yet remain ready for instant launch. Two new submarine classes are armed with such weapons, the US Los Angeles and the Soviet Oscar. Both classes are designed principally to attack opposing carrier task groups, but can also hit strategic ground targets.

The Los Angeles class is one of the most expensive additions to the US arsenal. Designated SSN, indicating that they are nuclear-powered hunter-killers, they are far bigger than any previous boat in this category and almost as big as the British Resolution class SSBNs. More than 50 are being built, despite their unit cost having more than trebled since they first entered service in 1976 (from $221m to $663m+).

Each Los Angeles displaces 6,100 tonnes (6,000 tons) on the surface and 7,010 tonnes (6,900 tons) submerged, and the boats' single-shaft 35,000shp (shaft horsepower) nuclear-powered turbines give them a submerged speed well in excess of 55km/h (30 knots). In addition to conventional weaponry the 22nd and subsequent boats have been fitted with 15 vertical launch tubes for the BGM-109A Tomahawk with nuclear warhead or the B/C/E variants with conventional 450kg (1,000lb) high-explosive charges. The earlier boats will be similarly retrofitted in due course. The A and C variants of Tomahawk have a range of up to 2,500km (1,550 miles), while the B and E are more tactical in nature with a range of 450km (280 miles).

The Soviet Oscar class vessels, as might be expected, are larger than the Los Angeles boats, with a displacement of 10,160 tonnes (10,000 tons) on the surface or 14,225 tonnes (14,000 tons) submerged. As in the Typhoon class, two nuclear reactors and twin shafts are employed to give a submerged speed in excess of 55km/h (30 knots). The use of this arrangement further enhances the survivability of Soviet submarines in a war environment, since they can still function with one shut-down reactor or damaged shaft. The boats are fitted with 12 vertical launch tubes for the SS-N-19 cruise missile, all details of which are currently speculative, though it is believed to have a

BELOW Artist's impression of a Soviet SS-NX-21 cruise missile in flight.

range in the region of 500km (300 miles). Whether the guidance technology in Soviet cruise missiles is as accurate as that in US designs is also unknown.

SURFACE-LAUNCHED CRUISE MISSILES

The SS-N-19 is also fitted to Kirov class rocket cruisers, two of which have so far been built with at least one more under construction. These large, 30,000 tonne (28,000-ton) vessels contain launchers for 20 cruise missiles as well as a variety of other, more conventional weapons. They have twin nuclear reactors plus an independent steam turbine system and their twin shafts give a maximum speed of over 55km/h (30 knots). Their wide range of armament, discussed in more detail below, gives them a formidable capability against carrier task groups, submarines and strategic land targets. They also carry at least three Kamov Ka-25 Hormone helicopters equipped with special electronic gear to enable them to provide mid-course corrections to the cruise missiles, so enhancing their accuracy.

In response to the threat posed by the *Kirov* and her sister ships, the US Navy is busily equipping its Ticonderoga, Virginia and Spruance classes with Tomahawk, and has already installed the missile on the old Iowa class battleships. These four magnificent vessels

ABOVE Soviet Oscar class cruise missile-armed nuclear attack submarine. The sheer bulk of Russian boats compared with American ones, because of their double hulls, is very obvious.

were all built during World War II and saw action at the end of the Pacific campaign. Subsequently they were mothballed, but USS *New Jersey* was recommissioned during the Vietnam War so that her 406mm (16in) guns could be used to give fire support to ground operations. *New Jersey* also saw action during the American intervention in the Lebanon in 1984, by which time her three sister ships were also being refurbished and modernized. Part of this programme includes the installation of eight Tomahawk cruise missile launchers.

The Iowa class ships are the last true battleships in service and almost certainly the last that will ever be built. They are sleekly massive, weighing in at 61,500 tonnes (58,000 tons), with four geared turbines providing 212,000shp to drive them through the water at 61km/h (33 knots). Heavily armoured above and below the waterline – unlike modern warships, which are hardly armoured at all – their most striking characteristics are the three awe-inspiring main gun turrets, two forward and one aft, each housing three 406mm (16in)

RIGHT One of the 406mm (16in) guns letting fly aboard the recommissioned battleship USS *New Jersey*. These magnificent vessels are being retrofitted with Tomahawk.

weapons, and a towering superstructure festooned with all manner of modern radio and microwave detectors and communications gear.

For secondary armament the Iowas have between 12 and 20 127mm (5in) guns and eight Harpoon anti-ship missile launchers as well as a variety of short-range anti-aircraft weapons. While lacking the modern refinements in some areas of the Kirov class rocket cruisers, they are potent weapons systems indeed, even if they do require crews of 1,600 men.

INTERCONTINENTAL BALLISTIC MISSILES (ICBMs)

Until the introduction of computerized inertial guidance systems and accurate navigation satellites enabled long-range ballistic missiles to be deployed effectively aboard submarines, such missiles had to be land-based. Their launch pads, no matter how deeply buried and protected, are static targets whose location will be programmed with minute accuracy into hostile missiles, which is why the main burden of carrying strategic nuclear missiles has moved from land to sea. Nevertheless, land-based ICBMs continue to form a major part of the arsenals of East and West.

US ICBM INSTALLATIONS

The principal American ICBMs since 1967 have been the Minuteman II and III, supplemented more recently by Peacekeeper (formerly known as MX), and the last six squadrons of elderly Titan IIs were finally phased out in 1987. The 450 Minuteman IIs, each with a single 1-2MT warhead, are deployed at Ellsworth, Malmstrom and Whiteman Air Force Bases (AFBs) while the 550 Minuteman IIIs, which have either three 200kT or two 300kT MIRVs, are based at Grand Forks, Malmstrom and Minot, all close to the Canadian border; 100 Peacekeeper missiles are being deployed in former Minuteman silos at Warren AFB.

Command of the ICBM force is exercised either from the National Military Command Center (NMCC) buried deep beneath the Pentagon in Washington, DC, or the alternative NMCC at Fort Ritchie in Maryland. The associated satellite communications and navigational equipment to provide mid-course guidance corrections are at the North American Air Defense (NORAD) headquarters buried half a kilometre (1,640ft) under Cheyenne

BELOW A Harpoon anti-shipping missile leaves its launch tube during an exercise.

Mountain in Colorado. A new space command base is being constructed nearby.

Since all the command centres are static installations which would obviously be the focal points for a Soviet nuclear attack and might not survive, four Boeing 747 airliners have been rebuilt as National Emergency Airborne Command Posts. These aircraft, which are normally based at Offut AFB in Nebraska, are divided into six sections: the National Command Authorities area, a conference room, briefing room, battle staff area, communications control centre and a rest area. The aircraft can be refueled in flight and can stay airborne for up to 72 hours. They are shielded against nuclear radiation and carry highly complex communications equipment allowing them to transmit orders and receive reports from other

■ **RIGHT** Part of the complex electronic command and control system inside an E-4 National Emergency Airborne Command Post.

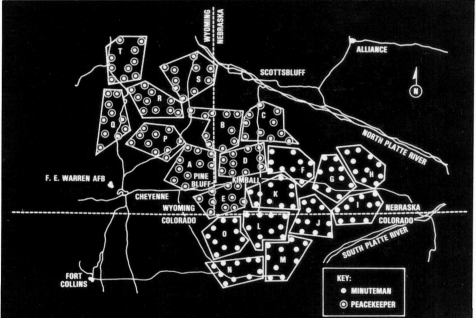

ABOVE Map showing the deployment of Peacekeeper and Minuteman missile silos at Warren AFB sprawling across the state line from Wyoming into Colorado.

LEFT One of the four Boeing National Emergency Airborne Command Posts.

aircraft, ground headquarters, warships and even submerged submarines.

The Minuteman and Peacekeeper missiles themselves are housed in hardened underground silos built to resist a pressure of 13,790kPa (2,000psi), which means they could survive an 18MT burst roughly 600m (660yd) away or a 1MT burst as close as 250m (275yd) away. (These figures are based on tests using conventional high explosives against scale models – the real thing has not been practised). The silos are dispersed over a very wide area – up to 46,600km^2 (18,000 sq miles) – and each silo is protected against sabotage within a fenced-in hectare (2.47 acres) of land liberally strewn with sensors to detect intruders. The silos themselves are 25m (82ft) deep and 4m (13ft) in diameter and protected by a 100-tonne (94ton) hexagonal shell.

Each flight of 10 missiles is controlled from a command capsule at least 5km (3 miles) away buried 15m (50ft) under the ground and mounted on shock absorbers. Each capsule is manned by two Air Force officers, and in the event of an attack a loudspeaker would emit a warning warble whereupon the men would immediately close the blast doors and turn on the internal air supply. Verification of the attack would take the form of the words 'Gentlemen, you have received an authorized launch instruction from the National Command Authority', accompanied by a coded printout on the telex machine. This printout has to match another sealed in a wall safe.

The two officers would then sit at their chairs, which are placed at right angles to each other 4.5m (15ft) apart, and simultaneously insert their keys into their consoles, turning them at the same time and holding them turned for two seconds. To prevent accidental firing the same operation has to be performed simultaneously by another two men in a second command capsule. Once launched, the missiles cannot be stopped, since the risk of an enemy learning an auto-destruct code prohibits the use of such a procedure.

WESTERN ICBMs

Minuteman is a three-stage solid-fueled missile which is hot-launched – in other words, the first rocket stage ignites inside the silo, the blast being deflected outside through vents in its base. The first stage burns for one minute,

providing 91,000kg (200,000lb) of thrust, then the second stage takes over to add another 27,200kg (60,000lb); finally, the third stage provides 16,000kg (35,000lb) to take the missile into its long sub-orbital trajectory over the North Pole. Reportedly accurate to within 220m (240yd), the missile has a maximum range of 12,875km (8,000 miles). In-flight guidance is provided where necessary by a fleet of nine EC-135C Airborne Launch Control aircraft, each of which is capable of independently tracking 200 missiles.

Peacekeeper, end-product of the hugely expensive but ultimately abortive MX programme of the 1970s, is a four-stage solid-fueled missile. Unlike Minuteman, it is cold-launched, which means that it is ejected from the silo by compressed gas before the first-stage rocket ignites. In theory, this means the silo is undamaged by the launch and could be reloaded, though it seems unlikely that anyone would be around to do the reloading.

MX was originally planned as a mobile system with the missiles moved by road from one underground location to another. The idea was that, by using dummy transporters as well, the actual locations of the real missiles from day to day could be concealed from satellite surveillance. It was an over-ambitious and hugely expensive programme which would have ended up costing over $5,000 million (at 1982 prices), and in the end President Reagan abandoned the mobile aspect, merely retaining 100 Peacekeeper missiles at refurbished (but, surprisingly, not reinforced) silos at Warren AFB. Installation of the missiles started in 1986 and is expected to be completed by 1990.

ABOVE The independently targetted warheads from two Minuteman III ICBMs head for targets in the Pacific Ocean during tests. The warheads were not 'live'!

ABOVE The independent warheads in the nose cone of a Peacekeeper missile. Up to ten can be carried depending on size.

Details of Peacekeeper are predictably scarcer than those of the older Minuteman system, but the new missile is reported as carrying 10 330kT MIRVs to a range of at least 11,100km (7,000 miles).

The only other Western country to have an independent ICBM force is France, whose SSBS (Sol-Sol Ballistique Stratégique) S-3 is the product of entirely home-grown technology. The first of 18 entered service in 1980, and the missiles are deployed in hardened silos at two sites in southern France, close to the Alps. They carry single 1.2MT warheads to a distance of 3,000km (1,865 miles).

SOVIET ICBMs

The Soviet Union has three principal ICBM systems, apart from the SS-20. The SS-17, -18 and -19 are emplaced in hardened silos which, Western experts have concluded, are probably stronger than the Minuteman/Peacekeeper installations, their ability to withstand up to 41,400kPa (6,000psi) being a necessity given the greater accuracy of the US warheads.

Control is officially in the hands of the RSVN (Raketnyye Voyska Strategicheskovo Naznacheniya, or Strategic Rocket Forces), but is actually shared by the KGB, a fact which helps deter any unauthorized launch attempt. This dual command structure means that Soviet strategic missile forces are generally maintained at a lower state of readiness than their American equivalents, and retargeting is said to take as long as 24 hours against half an hour for a Minuteman III.

Launch sites are concentrated in European Russia from the Caspian Sea westwards and strung out along the line of the Trans-Siberian Railway, with a further concentration along the border with China, where they are within range of Japan. The locations of Soviet command centres may be known in Intelligence circles but are not published, though the principal one is said to lie within 130km (80 miles) of Moscow. Airborne command posts are also employed in the form of the Tupolev Tu-126 and Ilyushin Il-76, details of whose internal arrangements are unknown.

The SS-18 is the oldest and largest of Soviet ICBMs, and the largest in the world since the withdrawal from service of the US Titan IIs. It is a two-stage liquid-fueled missile carrying, according to variant – of which there are four – anything from a single massive 20MT warhead to 10 500kT MIRVs. As they have demonstrated with their space technology, the Soviets tend to view size, power and simplicity as the answer to qualitative superiority, and their warheads are bigger than those carried by US missiles because they are less accurate. Despite its size and 78,000kg (172,000lb) weight, the SS-18 is a cold-launch weapon; its exact range is unknown, but it is obviously capable of reaching any target in the continental United States. Some 308 SS-18s are believed to be in service.

Since the 1970s, the SS-18 has been supplemented by the shorter-ranged but more versatile SS-17 and -19. The former is also a cold-launch vehicle while the latter is hot-launched, but the -19 appears to be the better system because some 360 are in service compared with less than half that number of -17s. The SS-17 is a two-stage liquid-fueled missile with a range of 11,000km (6,835 miles) and a payload of between four and six 200kT MIRVs. The SS-19 is also liquid-fueled, with a range estimated at 10,000km+ (6,200+ miles) and the vehicle carries six 500kT MIRVs. SS-17s and -19s are deployed mainly in western Russia, while the SS-18s are sited around the more central location of Tyuratam.

AIR-LAUNCHED NUCLEAR WEAPONS

Despite predictions of its demise going back more than 30 years, the long-range manned strategic bomber is still with us. By early 1988 the last of four squadrons of the US Air Force's Rockwell B-1B was becoming operational, while on the other side of the globe an estimated 250+ Tupolev Tu-22M Backfires and an unknown number of the even newer Blackjack were already in service.

All three new bombers are very advanced swing-wing aircraft carrying potent stand-off weapons – the American AGM-86B ALCM (air-launched cruise missile) and the Soviet AS-4 and AS-6 air-to-surface missiles or the new AS-X-15 cruise missile. Many other aircraft are nuclear-capable, including the F-111, Tornado and Mirage IV, and we shall encounter these later. For now, though, let us look at strategic aircraft, those capable of attacking the enemy's homelands from their own home bases.

THE B-1B

The Rockwell B-1B, the first prototype of which flew in 1974, was canceled by President Carter and revived by Ronald Reagan; it has taken a quarter of a century to get into service and the cost of the 100 examples built has been estimated at $40 billion. In its final configuration, however, it is a superb aircraft, the design of its fuselage, wings and engine intakes presenting a low profile to enemy radars, while radar-reflective paint as used on the SR-71 and TR-1 spyplanes further reduces its detectability.

Indeed, to a radar the B-1B appears only one-hundredth the size of a Boeing B-52, the aircraft which since the mid-1950s has been the mainstay of the US Air Force's Strategic Air Command (SAC). Even so, the USAF regards it as an interim design pending the introduction of the Northrop Advanced Technology Bomber (ATB), employing all the latest 'stealth' technology, in the 1990s.

The B-1B's four 13,563kg (29,900lb) static thrust turbofans give it a speed of around Mach 1.5 at 11,000m (36,000ft), but its planned cruise speed en route to a target is around 950-1,000km/h (590-620mph) (just subsonic); at such speeds it has a range of some 12,000km (7,500 miles). The aircraft can carry up to 22 cruise missiles, which have a range of some 1,200km (750 miles), but would normally carry a proportion of other weapons for self-defence in hostile airspace.

The B-1B is designed for low-altitude penetration missions, only using its top speed on afterburners and undisclosed maximum ceiling to escape the target area after it has released its stand-off missiles. It has enormously complex offensive and defensive electronic systems, and can operate from comparatively short runways.

BELOW The B-1A has paved the way for the B-1B operational bomber, offering with its lower radar signature the real possibility of penetrating enemy airspace at high subsonic speed and very low level.

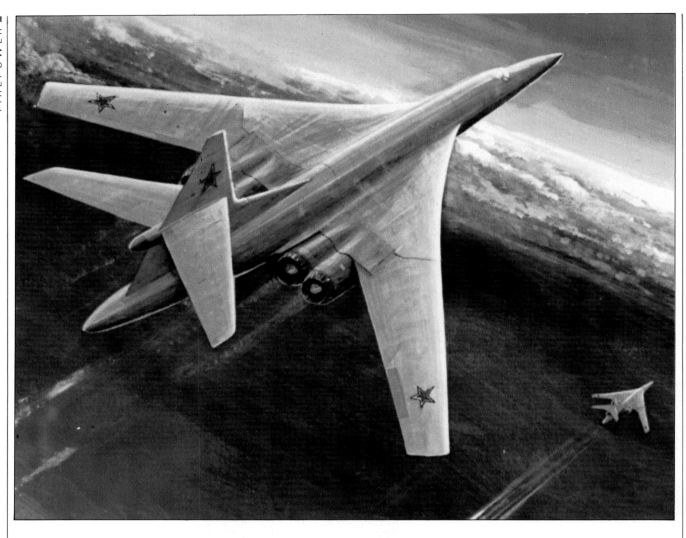

BACKFIRE AND BLACKJACK

As with most modern Soviet military designs, little positive is known about the new bomber codenamed Backfire by NATO, not even its designation, which could be Tu-22M or Tu-26. First flown in the late 1960s or early 1970s and progressively modernized ever since, it is a large swing-wing aircraft bearing a superficial resemblance to the American F-111. Powered by two afterburning turbofans rated at approximately 20,000kg (44,100lb) static thrust each, it is faster than the B-1B – its top speed at 11,000m (36,000ft) is in the region of 2,125km/h (1,320mph) – but on active operations it would use a similar high subsonic speed at low level. Range is less than half that of the B-1B at 5,500km (3,400 miles), though in-flight refueling could double that figure. Like most Soviet bombers, the Backfire retains a tail armament of twin remote-controlled 23mm guns, an arrangement long since considered

obsolete in the West although still retained on the B-52. The aircraft has modern ECM systems and carries a fourth crew member as an electronic warfare specialist.

Even less is known in the West about the aircraft codenamed Blackjack, which was first observed by an American spy satellite in 1981. It is provisionally labelled a Tupolev design but no model number has been discovered. It is a

BELOW LEFT Tu-22M/Tu-26 Backfire bomber with an AS-4 Kitchen nuclear missile beneath its fuselage.

ABOVE Artist's impression of the Tupolev Blackjack, Soviet equivalent of the B-1.

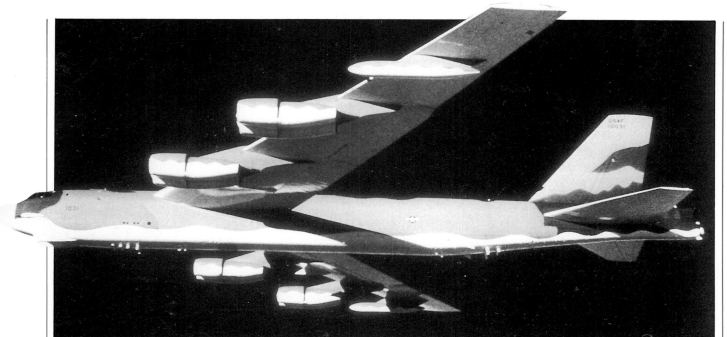

four-engined swing-wing aircraft, like the B-1B, but is both larger and faster, performance being given as 2,225km/h (1,380mph) at high altitude while range without in-flight refueling is estimated at 7,300km (4,500 miles). The engines are believed to be turbofans in the 22,000kg (48,500lb) static thrust class, but actual performance and potential remain unknown.

Both Backfire and Blackjack can carry a wide range of ordnance, from conventional bombs to cruise missiles. Their most important weapons are the AS-4 liquid-propelled rocket with a 350kT warhead, the AS-6 solid-fueled anti-ship missile, also with a 350kT warhead, and the new AS-X-15 cruise missile, airborne version of the naval SS-NX-21. Respective ranges are 460km (285 miles), 250km (155 miles) and 3,000km (1,865 miles), and the combination of Blackjack and AS-X-15 could reach any target in the world.

OLDER STRATEGIC BOMBERS

The only other strategic bombers still in service are the American B-52 and the Soviet Tu-95 Bear, both of which are now very long in the tooth, and since the retirement of the last of Britain's Avro Vulcan fleet in 1986 no other country possesses long-range aircraft. The B-52, which proved so vulnerable to surface-to-air missiles in Vietnam, was designed during the tense early years of the Cold War and first became operational in 1955. It has been con-

stantly updated ever since and the latest fit for the B-52Gs and Hs still in service is 12 AGM-86B cruise missiles either on four triple under-wing pylons or in a rotary bay in the fuselage; other armament options include the Harpoon anti-ship cruise missile, SRAM (Short Range Attack Missile), MRASM (Medium Range Air-to-Surface Missile) or up to 40,400kg (89,000lb) of conventional bombs.

The B-52 is powered by eight 6,237kg (13,750lb) (G) or 7,711kg (17,000lb) (H) turbine engines for a maximum speed of 957km/h (595mph) without underwing stores at 14,000m (46,000ft). Range varies according to load carried but is typically 13,500-15,300km (8,400-9,500 miles). As noted above, four 12.7mm (0.5in) or one 20mm gun are in a remotely controlled tail barbette. Despite their age some 260 B-52s are still operational in the United States and many more are mothballed against any future emergency. However, despite advances in ECM equipment, the aircraft's enormous size and high radar profile would make it immensely vulnerable in any modern war.

The same is true of the Soviet Union's Tu-95/Tu-142 Bear, the G version of which is equipped to carry the AS-4 350kT missile; earlier models still in service can carry free-fall nuclear weapons and the C model can launch the AS-6 anti-ship missile. This enormous aircraft is powered by four immense turboprops driving contra-rotating propellers which give

ABOVE A B-52H bomber of Strategic Air Command. Their age and large radar signature would make these aircraft very vulnerable in a major war – rather like trying to take a Handley Page 0/400 over Berlin in 1940!

it a cruising speed of 700km/h (435mph) at around 13,000m (43,000ft) and an unrefueled range with full weapons load in excess of 16,500km (10,250 miles).

The Tu-95 has six 23mm guns for self-defence in three remotely controlled barbettes, one in the tail, one below the lower rear fuselage and one on top of the fuselage slightly further forward; ECM equipment varies according to version but is believed to be extremely sophisticated. Latest version of the Tu-142 is the Bear-H, specifically designed to carry the AS-X-15 cruise missile, which extends the weapon system's effective range to any spot in the world.

BATTLEFIELD WEAPONS

So designated because they are designed principally for tactical use against enemy armoured formations, battlefield nuclear weapons are short-range nuclear missiles launched from relatively small mobile carriers. With SS-12 and Pershing II being removed under the Reagan/Gorbachov agreement the only remaining operational types will be Lance and Pluton.

The US Lance is a small, short-range missile which can carry a normal 10kT or an enhanced radiation (neutron) warhead, or a 454kg (1,000lb) high-explosive charge. It is in service not just with the US Army but also with the ground forces of Britain, Belgium, Holland, Italy, West Germany and Israel, though in Europe only the British and American weapons carry nuclear warheads and none of them are of the enhanced radiation type. It is likely that the Israelis also have the capability to fit nuclear warheads, but this is something they will neither confirm nor deny.

Lance is specifically designed to break up massed tank formations at a range of between 70km and 120km (43-75 miles) and is deployed in large numbers, more than 2,000 having entered service since 1972. It is carried on the M752 fully-tracked TEL vehicle derived from the M113 armoured personnel carrier, which is fully amphibious. In action, the M752 would be accompanied by two M688s, each carrying two further missiles for reloading.

The French Pluton, which carries either a 25kT standard nuclear warhead or a 15kT enhanced radiation weapon, is slightly larger than Lance but has the same maximum range of 120km (75 miles). The carrier vehicle is a greatly modified AMX-30 tank chassis and hull, only 30 of which are currently in service, but they can quickly be reloaded in the field. Pluton is

ABOVE A Tu-95, used variously for ocean reconnaissance and missile carrying.

FAR RIGHT The French Pluton tactical battlefield missile on its tracked launcher; Pluton can carry either an AN 51 warhead or a smaller 10kt warhead.

RIGHT Lance, the British Army's tactical surface-to-surface guided missile, mounted on an amphibious M133 tracked carrier.

due to be replaced by a new vertical-launch system on a wheeled semi-trailer vehicle: called Hades, this will have three times the range of the existing missile and will carry an enhanced radiation warhead of between 10 and 25kT.

ENHANCED RADIATION WEAPONS

Enhanced radiation weapons work by emitting a far greater quantity of 'hard' radiation in the form of neutrons than is released by a normal nuclear warhead. Whereas the latter achieves its effect principally through heat and blast, 80 per cent of a neutron bomb's yield is radiation. This minimizes damage to structures such as tanks and buildings but would kill everyone inside and knock out all electronic equipment. Comparing a 10kT conventional nuclear weapon and a 1kT neutron bomb air burst at 100m (330ft), for example, the former would flatten all buildings out to some 1,500m (1,640yd) from ground zero (the point directly below the detonation), but the latter would leave them undamaged at 500m (550yd). More significantly, while the crew of a modern main battle tank would have an excellent chance of surviving the 10kT burst at 500m even though their vehicle would be badly damaged, the radiation from the neutron bomb would kill them all out to 1,500m.

Because of these effects the United States and the Soviet Union have agreed to suspend further development of enhanced radiation weapons: if they were to be widely deployed they could encourage aggression by encouraging one side to attempt to knock out the other's armour in a pre-emptive strike. France has unilaterally retained the weapon on the grounds that, not being a full partner in NATO, it will only use nuclear weapons in retaliation against a first strike.

Everyone hopes that nuclear weapons will never again be used in anger. A full-scale global conflict would leave precious few survivors, and even they would not escape the long-term effects of radiation. For this reason there is a continued need for conventional land, sea and air forces both to preserve the status quo and to serve in the limited wars which have proliferated since 1945.

2

FIREPOWER
AT SEA

Given that ballistic-missile submarines are the principal strategic weapon, it is natural that naval weapon systems designed to seek out and destroy them enjoy high priority in all the world's navies. The main enemy of an SSBN is an SSN or SSK – that is, a nuclear or conventionally powered attack submarine – and a detailed look at a representative example will help set the scene.

A TYPICAL SUBMARINE

Right in the bow is the forward-looking sonar transducer array, surrounded in Western boats by ballast tanks which control rate of dive and ascent. (Soviet submarines, being double-skinned, have ballast tanks grouped all round the vessel.) This forward area also contains the anchor and chains, and the outlet shutters for the torpedo tubes. The tubes themselves pierce the main pressure hull, whose hemispherical front lies behind the forward space, and whose top has a hatch through which torpedoes are loaded. The forward compartment also houses the hydroplanes, which control the angle of the submarine's dive or ascent.

Immediately behind the forward end of the pressure hull is a compartment containing the forward escape tower, and below this is the torpedo compartment itself, where the weapons are loaded ready for use. Behind another watertight bulkhead lies the crew accommodation section, torpedo storage area, galley, messrooms and further sonar gear, and aft of these the sail (formerly known as the conning tower) rises out of the pressure hull. The sail contains a navigation platform (bridge), attack and surveillance periscopes, one or more radomes, EW and ECM antennas and, in the case of non-nuclear boats, a snorkel and diesel exhaust. In some classes of submarine diving planes are mounted on the sides of the sail instead of the bow.

Directly below the sail is the control room, and the adjacent communications centre. There is a control room hatch behind the sail, along with further crew accommodation and auxiliary machinery, and at about the mid-point of the vessel's hull comes the pressurized water-cooled nuclear reactor. Behind this at the top of the hull is the reactor control room, with the auxiliary diesel generator below it, and further aft again lies the engine room with its turbine leading to the drive shaft and propeller. Right

at the stern are the after hydroplanes and twin rudders. Numerous apertures dot the hull – access and escape hatches, water vents for cooling, special hatches to emit communications buoys, and so on. SSBNs are broadly similar, but with an additional compartment in the middle housing the missiles.

HUNTER-KILLER SUBMARINES

SSNs and SSKs are tasked both with hunting and killing hostile submarines and surface warships and with defending friendly SSBNs and carrier task groups against unfriendly submarines of the same type. They are extremely versatile weapon systems, very fast, very quiet – and very deadly, a fact whose recognition by the Soviet Union in the 1960s has enabled it to maintain an advantage ever since.

Soviet submarines pose a threat not only to American, British and French SSBNs and to surface warships, but also to the economically vital sealanes of the world. As a result, the concept of a nuclear war fought almost entirely at sea, between naval task forces and convoys, has increasingly exercised professional wargamers in Washington, Moscow, London and elsewhere in recent years.

The average submerged speed of a modern SSN is in excess of 55km/h (30knots) and the fastest of all, the Soviet Alfas, are capable of better than 75km/h (40 knots). Such vessels can dive to depths of 400m (1,300ft) – even more in the case of the Alfas and the American Los Angeles class – and while most are constructed of steel or steel alloys the latest Soviet submarines of the Alfa and Mike classes are made

ABOVE The weapons control panels for the Harpoon and Tigerfish torpedoes aboard the submarine HMS Trafalgar.

OPPOSITE A Sea Harrier just airborne from HMS *Invincible*. The Sea King helicopter hovering in the background is present to try to rescue the pilot in case of a mishap on take-off.

of titanium. Titanium is far more expensive and difficult to work than steel, but it can withstand higher water pressures, enabling such boats to dive to 900m (2,950ft) and more. Moreover, a titanium hull does not reveal its presence to a magnetic anomaly detector.

One of the reasons conventional diesel-powered attack submarines have been kept in use, apart from their relatively low cost, is that they are intrinsically quieter than nuclear-powered boats. The latter require noisy pumps handling large quantities of water to cool their reactors even when they are lying stationary in the water, and stealth is the key to underwater success.

RIGHT A Los Angeles class SSN, USS *Providence* at speed on the surface.

TORPEDOES

Despite the introduction of submarine-launched anti-ship missiles the torpedo remains the principal armament of the attack submarine. For some time the 533mm (21in) torpedo has been standard around the world, representing the best compromise between overall size and warhead capacity. While older designs were free-running, modern systems are wire-guided, with a passive sonar head which transmits its readings back to the parent submarine so that guidance corrections can be applied. When it is evident that the target vessel has detected the torpedo the sonar switches to the active mode and automatically homes in.

The Royal Navy's Mk 24 Tigerfish is representative of modern torpedoes. Propelled by an electric motor at 83km/h (45 knots) to a max-

ABOVE The bulbous sail of a Soviet Alpha class attack submarine, the fastest boats in the world.

imum range of 35km (22 miles), Tigerfish has now virtually replaced the old Mk 8 torpedo, a salvo of which sank the Argentinian cruiser *Belgrano* during the Falklands conflict. Although its warhead size is classified, it must be substantial. Even so, a torpedo has to catch its target first, and the very high speeds of modern Soviet submarines make this a difficult task. A new British torpedo called Spearfish will have a speed of some 150km/h (80 knots), and similar weapons are under development in the USA and USSR.

OTHER ANTI-SUBMARINE WEAPONS

The traditional torpedo is supplemented nowadays by submarine-launched missiles such as Sub-Harpoon, an American weapon also used by the Royal Navy, which is designed to attack surface ASW warships. It is housed in a capsule which is launched by compressed air from the submarine's torpedo tubes: as it breaks the surface the cap automatically blows off the capsule and a booster rocket takes the missile clear of the surface. When the booster burns out it is discarded, and after reaching an apogee of 1,500m (4,920ft) the missile descends toward the surface again and a sustainer motor takes over.

Sub-Harpoon is pre-programmed with the location of the target vessel at the time of launch, but mid-course corrections can be transmitted either by the submarine (which risks revealing the vessel's location) or by a friendly aircraft in the vicinity. When the missile nears its target its own active sensor head becomes operative and guides it straight to the enemy vessel, which it hits at the waterline. Sub-Harpoon flies at a high subsonic speed just above the waves, making it extremely difficult to detect or intercept, and its range is given as 96km (60 miles).

SUBROC (submarine rocket) is a similar American system designed specifically for use against submerged enemy submarines. It is also launched by compressed air from a torpedo tube, and at a safe distance from the parent vessel its solid fuel rocket motor ignites, taking it to the surface and then to a high supersonic speed. When the motor burns out it separates from the 1kT nuclear depth bomb warhead, which descends by parachute and detonates at a preset depth. The missile's range is 56km (35 miles) and, because of the massive concussion

effect of a nuclear explosion underwater, the relatively tiny warhead will definitely destroy any submarine within 5km (3 miles) and stands a good chance of doing so out to 8km (5 miles). The Soviet equivalent of SUBROC is the SS-N-15/16 which has effectively identical range and capability.

Although the Tomahawk cruise missile was specifically designed to fit into standard 533m (21in) torpedo tubes, the US Navy has fitted fifteen vertical-launch tubes in the bow casing of later Los Angeles class boats because the missiles occupied space that was needed for conventional torpedo stowage. In its non-nuclear anti-ship variants, Tomahawk has over twice the range of Sub-Harpoon and a warhead nearly double the size, making it effective against larger surface vessels such as rocket cruisers and aircraft carriers. The same is true

of the Soviet cruise missiles described in the previous chapter. Even then, it is estimated that around eight cruise missiles with high-explosive warheads would be needed to sink a large fleet carrier.

The final anti-submarine weapon deployed by submarines is the mine. This too is designed to fit standard torpedo tubes, and modern mines carry acoustic, magnetic and electrical sensors to detect the passage of an enemy submarine. A recent development in this field is the US Navy's CAPTOR (an acronym for encapsulated torpedo) which comprises a standard Mk 46 torpedo laid in a capsule equipped with sensors. When the capsule senses the proximity of an enemy submarine it automatically fires the torpedo. Such systems are almost impossible

OPPOSITE A Sub-Harpoon anti-shipping missile breaks free of its launching container as it reaches the surface.

ABOVE Accelerating rapidly, a SUBROC submarine-launched anti-submarine missile also clears the water.

RIGHT The torpedo control panel aboard the British SSN HMS *Trafalgar*.

BELOW An artist's impression of one of the new Soviet Mike class attack submarines.

OPPOSITE The crowded confines of the engine room aboard a German Type 209 class SSK.

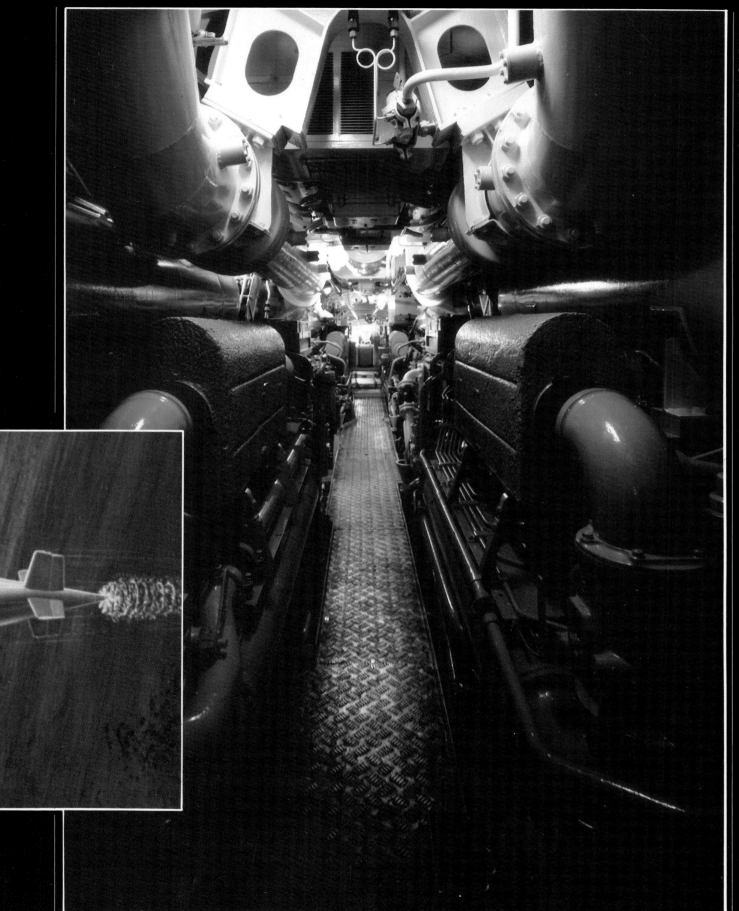

*Surface displacement; submerged figure unavailable but probably circa 2,400 tons.

Submarine Type/name	Country of Origin	DIMENSIONS (M)			Submerged displacement (tons)	Submerged speed (knots)	Weapons
		Length	Beam	Draught			
Alfa SSN	Russia	79.3	10.0	7.6	3,800	40+	6 × 533m tubes
Agosta SSK	France	67.6	6.8	5.4	1,725	20	4 × 533m tubes
Kilo SSK	Russia	70.0	9.0	7.0	3,200	?	8 × 533mm tubes
Näcken SSK	Sweden	49.5	5.6	5.6	1,125	20	6 × 533mm + 2 × 406mm tubes
Los Angeles SSN	America	109.7	10.1	9.8	6,900	30+	Harpoon, Tomahawk, 4 × 533mm tubes
Mike SSN	Russia	110	?	?	9,700	40+	SS-N-21, 6 × 533mm tubes
Rubis SSN	France	72.1	7.6	6.4	2,670	25	SM.39, 4 × 533mm tubes
Tango SSK	Russia	92.0	9.0	7.0	3,700	16	8 × 533mm tubes
Trafalgar SSN	Britain	85.4	9.83	9.5	5,208	30+	Sub-Harpoon, 6 × 533mm tubes
Type 209 SSK	West Germany	54.4	6.2	5.5	1,210	23	8 × 533mm tubes
Upholder SSK	Britain	70.3	7.6	5.5	2,400	20	Sub-Harpoon, Stonefish, 6 × 533mm tubes
Victor III SSN	Russia	104.0	10.0	7.3	6,000	30	SS-N-15, SS-NX-16, 6 × 533mm tubes
Walrus SSK	Netherlands	66.2	10.3	7.1	2,350	20	6 × 533mm tubes
Yuushio SSK	Japan	76.0	9.9	7.5	2,200*	20	6 × 533mm tubes

to detect until it is too late, and in time of war they would be laid at vital choke points, such as the Greenland–Iceland–UK gap.

OTHER SSNs

Apart from the American Los Angeles class already described, the principal SSNs in service are the Soviet Alfa, Mike and Victor III, the British Trafalgar and the French Rubis classes. The Victor III is the oldest of the Soviet boats and 18 are believed to be still in service; it has a single reactor and shaft developing 30,000shp to give it a maximum speed of 55km/h (30 knots) under water. Weapons carried in addition to torpedoes are the SS-N-15 and SS-NX-16, and the same systems are deployed aboard the more modern Alfa class, while the even more recent Mike boats can also carry the SS-NX-21 cruise missile.

The Alfas are comparatively small vessels, which suggests the use of a more compact nuclear reactor than normal, and perhaps one cooled by a liquid metal such as sodium. (American experiments with sodium cooling were unsuccessful but may be taken up again because the elimination of the need for water cooling reduces a submarine's sound signature considerably.) Six Alfas have been built so far: they have a single shaft rated at 45,000shp which gives them a dived speed in excess of 75km/h (40 knots). Little is known about the new Mike class boats except their titanium construction.

The Royal Navy's Trafalgar class boats, which will eventually number seven, are a logical development of the earlier Swiftsure, Valiant and Churchill classes. The first was commissioned in 1983, and they are armed with Tigerfish and Sub-Harpoon. Said to be the quietest SSNs in service anywhere, they are powered by a single nuclear reactor driving twin turbines connected to a single shaft, which gives a top speed in excess of 55km/h (30 knots). The boats can dive to at least 500m (1,640ft) and have a complement of 97.

The French Rubis class boats, the first of which entered service in 1982, are the smallest SSNs in the world, displacing only 2,830 tonnes (2,670 tons) submerged. Their single shafts give them a speed of some 46km/h (25 knots) submerged, and they are armed with both conventional 533mm (21in) torpedoes and the SM.39 Exocet.

DIESEL-ELECTRIC SUBMARINES

SSKs – conventional diesel/electric powered submarines – are far too numerous to describe here individually. They include the French Agosta, Soviet Kilo and Tango, Swedish Näcken, Dutch Walrus, Japanese Yuushio and German Type 209 classes – the last have a unique minelaying 'bandolier' around their hulls – and the new British Upholder class, the first of which entered service in 1988, is taken as representative of a state-of-the-art SSK. An interesting point to note is that the US Navy has no operational non-nuclear boats left in service, a fact which tends to support the theory that in the event of a major war the US intends to carry the conflict to the enemy, for conventional submarines would only be of use in defending sealanes relatively close to the continental United States. To defend their own coastlines the Americans rely on surface vessels and aircraft, which might prove a mistake since the main enemy of one submarine is still another submarine.

HMS *Upholder* and her sisters, which will ultimately number 10, were designed to replace the elderly Oberon class boats which have been in service since 1962. She has a high-tensile single-skinned steel hull and a sail largely composed of glass reinforced plastic, and in overall shape closely resembles an SSN. However, she only costs half as much as an equivalent nuclear-powered boat, a point in favour of SSKs dismissed in the United States.

Upholder is driven by twin diesel generators of 3,025bhp and a single electric motor, giving her a surface speed of 22km/h (12 knots) and 37km/h (20 knots) dived. Range is restricted compared to the virtually unlimited endurance of a nuclear boat, but she can still stay at sea for up to 49 days without replenishment and can cover 4,630km (2,880 miles) without refueling. She carries both conventional and towed-array sonars, the latter, being separated from the ambient noises created by the boat herself, being particularly important in detecting enemy submarines. She has six 533mm (21in) bow tubes from which she can launch Tigerfish torpedoes, Sub-Harpoon missiles and Stonefish mines. Brief details of the SSKs mentioned above are given in the accompanying table, but it should be stressed that these are representative not exhaustive.

ABOVE Whereas Second World War ships might have a single radar display, modern vessels such as HMS *Invincible* – especially those designed to act as flagships to task groups – have dozens, all searching at different frequencies and ranges to pick up the slightest movement on or above the water.

AIRCRAFT CARRIERS

If the submarine is the principal weapon in the major navies of the world today, aircraft carriers remain the visible symbols of maritime strength and are still immensely powerful, if vulnerable, weapons platforms. Their enormous construction and running costs limit the numbers built but they provide great tactical flexibility, not least in anti-submarine warfare.

During World War II there were three carrier superpowers, the United States, Britain and Japan. Today there is only one – the United States – although under the inspired leadership of Admiral Sergei Gorshkov the Soviet Navy has in recent years closed the gap and there is every indication of a new and continuing building programme.

Britain no longer has any true aircraft carriers; construction of the Royal Navy's three Invincible class carriers was only authorized by a parsimonious parliament when they were euphemistically designated through-deck cruisers, and one of them would have been sold to Australia had not HMS *Invincible* herself proved so invaluable during the Falklands conflict. That war also demonstrated how valuable a conventional fleet carrier would have been, with its long-range strike and airborne early warning aircraft, but the last, *Ark Royal,* had been scrapped in 1978.

Outside the USA and USSR only France retains modern fleet carriers, though several elderly British and American vessels soldier on in the service of smaller navies. Italy and Spain are the only other countries with modern carriers, both Invincible type designed to operate Harriers and helicopters.

THE NIMITZ CLASS

The largest and most impressive of all carriers are those of the US Navy's Nimitz class, which will ultimately total six vessels in the 1990s. Together with the older *Enterprise,* the US Navy's first nuclear-powered carrier, and the conventional Forrestal and Kitty Hawk classes, this will result in a fleet of fifteen carriers, though the two elderly Midway class ships are now only used for training purposes.

At the heart of the *Nimitz* lie two A4W nuclear reactors each developing 130,000shp. Four steam turbines powered by the reactors drive four shafts to give the enormous vessel a top speed of 55km/h (30 knots). Range is effectively unlimited and the reactors only have to be powered down for servicing every 13 years.

Everything about the *Nimitz* is big. Her

BELOW A flight of Tomcats over the USS *Nimitz* in the Indian Ocean.

angled flight deck is 81.5m (267ft) long and 11m (36ft) wide, and even her crew complement is enormous – 3,151 officers and men to operate the ship and a further 2,625 men in her air wing.

Obviously, the ship's aircraft are her principal weapons. These normally comprise 24 F-14 Tomcats, 24 A-7E Corsairs, sixteen A-6 Intruders, four E-2C Hawkeyes, four EA-6B Prowlers, ten S-3A Vikings and six SH-3H Sea King

helicopters. In addition, she has a formidable array of missiles and guns, specifically the Sea Sparrow missile for intermediate range anti-aircraft defence and the Phalanx close-in weapon system to handle any missiles that might penetrate the outer fighter and missile screens.

The RIM-7H Sea Sparrows are housed in three launchers, each containing eight missiles. Introduced in 1977 as the replacement for the older RIM-7E, the RIM-7H is a semi-active homing missile with a range of 15km (9 miles); it has been adopted by several NATO navies. Phalanx is a six-barrel 20mm fast-firing gun which operates on the Gatling principle: with automatic radar guidance and a rate of fire of 3,000rds/min it is capable of shooting down cruise-type anti-ship missiles as well as aircraft.

ABOVE USS *Nimitz* with four F-14 Tomcats ranged for take-off and a variety of other aircraft parked at the stern.

BELOW A Tomcat in the foreground with an A-6E Intruder behind on the USS *Nimitz*.

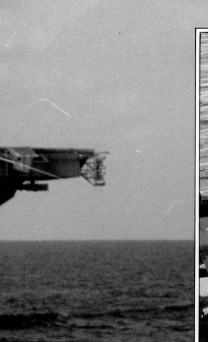

SOVIET AND UK CARRIERS

The Soviet Navy has no equivalent to the Nimitz class at present though at least one aircraft carrier, provisionally named *Kremlin* by NATO, is known to be building at a Black Sea yard. The new carrier is believed to be in the 80,000-tonne (75,000-ton) class, with nuclear power and an angled flight deck to accommodate the MiG-23 Flogger and MiG-29 Fulcrum. Until this vessel enters service the only Soviet carriers will be the four Kiev class ships, which have angled flight decks but only operate the Yak-38 Forger V/STOL aircraft, together with Ka-25 Hormone helicopters for anti-submarine warfare and missile guidance; 12 Forgers and 20 Hormones are carried. *Kiev* and her sister ships have conventional steam turbines developing 180,000shp and driving four shafts for a top speed of 58km/h (32 knots) and a range of 25,000km (15,500 miles). Useful in their own right, they also pave the way for

more ambitious things.

The Kiev class ships are of an unusual design which clearly indicates their primary role to be anti-submarine warfare. The superstructure and forecastle bristle with guns, missile launchers and torpedo tubes, including twin SUW-N-1 anti-submarine missile launchers containing an estimated twenty FRAS-1 missiles; these have a range of 30km (19 miles) and carry nuclear warheads. There are also two mortars to fire conventional depth charges and ten 533mm (21in) torpedo tubes.

For action against surface vessels *Kiev* carries eight triple launchers for SS-N-12s. These large missiles have a range of 460km (285 miles) and can carry either conventional high-explosive or nuclear warheads; mid-course guidance is provided by the helicopters. Finally, for anti-aircraft defence each ship has two twin SA-N-3 launchers containing a battery of 72 missiles. These have a range of 35km (22 miles) and are supplemented by 36 10km (6-mile) range SA-N-4s. For last-ditch defence against cruise missiles the ships carry four eight-barrel Gatling-type 30mm guns.

Britain's Invincible class carriers are far smaller than the Kievs, and their flight decks are not angled, but a ski jump forward extends the range of the Sea Harrier aircraft by reducing the power needed for takeoff. Between five and ten Harriers plus nine to twelve Sea King helicopters can be carried, four of the latter being Airborne Early Warning (AEW) machines since the Falklands experience. The vessels are powered by four gas turbines producing 112,000shp through two shafts; cruising range at 33km/h (18 knots) is 9,260km (5,750 miles), and this can be extended by replenishment at sea from a tanker.

For self-defence the Invincibles have a twin Sea Dart launcher, two Phalanx CIWS, two

TOP A MiG-23 of the Soviet Air Force during a goodwill visit to Finland recently. A navalized version will equip the new super-carrier *Kremlin*.

ABOVE The crowded fo'c's'le of the Russian carrier *Minsk* showing the missile and torpedo tubes.

AIRCRAFT CARRIERS

Carrier Name	Country of Origin	DIMENSIONS (M) Length	Beam	Draught	Displacement (tons)	Speed (knots)	Aircraft carried
Clemenceau	France	267	32.0	8.6	32,780	32	40 × Super Etendard, 2 × Super Frelon, 2 × Alouette, 1 × Alizé
Giuseppe Garibaldi	Italy	180.2	23.4	6.7	13,320	30	10 × Sea Harrier + 1 × Sh-3D or 16 × SH-3D
Invincible	Britain	206.6	31.9	7.3	19,810	28	5–10 × Sea Harrier, 9-12 × Sea King
Kiev	Russia	274.0	48.0	10.0	42,000	32	12 × Yak-38, 20 × Ka-25
Kitty Hawk	America	327.0	39.6	11.0	82,000	30	24 × F-14, 24 × A-7E, 14 × A/KA-6E/D, 4 × E-2C, 4 × EA-6B, 10 × S-3A, 6 × SH-3H
Nimitz	America	332.8	76.5	11.3	82,000	30	24 × F-14, 24 × A-7E, 16 × A-6, 4 × E-2C, 4 × EA-6B, 10 × S-3A, 6 × SH-3H
Principe de Asturias	Spain	196.0	24.4	9.1	14,700	26	6-8 AV-8B, 6-8 × Sea King, 8 × AB212

RIGHT Sea Harrier carrying a pair of Sea Eagle anti-shipping missiles.

BELOW The French carrier *Clemenceau* with two Super Frelon helicopters ranged on the flight deck aft and four Alouettes forward.

LEFT Launch of the Italian carrier *Garibaldi* in 1983.

BELOW A Dassault-Breguet Super Étendard attack fighter about to take off from the flight deck of the French carrier *Clemenceau*.

20mm Oerlikon guns and both American SRBOC and British Corvus countermeasures dispensers. The dispensers throw out a variety of forms of chaff to confuse incoming enemy missiles. Sea Dart is a lightweight anti-aircraft missile with a range of 30km (48 miles) which proved itself in the Falklands.

As carriers are normally the flagships in any naval task force they have elaborate computerized command, control and communications (C^3) equipment enabling them to monitor and control the movements of the other ships in the group. The accompanying table shows brief details of types in service.

CRUISERS

The cruiser, with firepower nearly equal to that of a battleship and the speed of a destroyer, has long been one of the most versatile of all warships, able to deliver a hefty punch or race away from superior opposition to fight again another day. Modern long-range anti-ship missiles obviously make cruisers more vulnerable, but in exchange they can themselves mete out heavier punishment.

The biggest and most impressive cruisers, the Soviet Navy's Kirov class battlecruisers, are more than twice as big as any Western cruisers. Constructed from 1980 onwards, these 30,000-tonne (28,000-ton) vessels are capable of single-handedly fighting an entire carrier task force with a reasonable chance of success. Propulsion is via two shafts powered by a combined nuclear and steam system which gives 120,000shp.

SOVIET CRUISERS

The Kirovs' main offensive armament is a battery of 20 SS-N-19 missiles in vertical launch tubes forward of the bridge superstructure. With a range that could be as high as 500km (310 miles) and nuclear warheads, these can be ripple-launched against a single large target or aimed individually against separate targets. Mid-flight guidance corrections are provided by three Ka-25 helicopters housed in a hangar toward the stern. The helicopters can also carry torpedoes for anti-submarine warfare, but the main ASW weapon is the twin SS-N-14 launcher housing 16 missiles with a range of 46km (29 miles) and, possibly, nuclear warheads. In addition, there are three mortars to fire conventional depth charges, and two banks

of five 533mm (21in) torpedo tubes.

For anti-aircraft defence the Kirovs have 12 launchers for SA-N-6 and two launchers for SA-N-4 missiles with ranges of 50km (30 miles) and 10km (6 miles) respectively, plus eight 30mm CIWS. In addition, *Kirov* has two single 100mm (4in) guns in individual turrets while the second ship in the class, *Frunze,* has a twin 130mm (5in) mounting. These vessels have equally impressive radar, sonar, electronic warfare and communications equipment enabling them to operate as flagships to naval task forces.

Complementing the Kirov class is the new Slava class, the name ship of which entered service in 1983. These general-purpose cruisers are powered by conventional gas turbines: the use of a non-nuclear power plant may be an economy measure. The ships are very sleek in appearance with extremely streamlined hulls and superstructures marred only by two rows of four twin SS-N-12 launcher tubes. A single Ka-25 helicopter is carried to provide mid-course guidance corrections for the missiles.

Secondary armament takes the form of eight SA-N-6 and two twin SA-N-4 anti-aircraft missile launchers and may include the new SA-N-7 intermediate-range missile as well. The SA-N-7 is believed to have a range of about 28km (17 miles). For a modern warship the *Slava* seems gun-heavy, having two twin 130mm (5in) turrets as well as six 30mm CIWS, but the use of naval firepower in support of amphibious landings is not something the Soviet Navy is likely to have neglected in its calculations. There are also two mortars and eight torpedo tubes, a combination which gives the vessels considerable firepower to expend against enemy surface vessels and good self-defence against aerial attack.

Supplementing the Kirov and Slava classes are the six dedicated anti-submarine cruisers of the Udaloy class and the new general-purpose Sovremenny class, of which five have been built so far. The main armament of the Udaloys is two quadruple launchers for SS-N-14 missiles, eight SA-N-8 anti-aircraft missile launchers, two 100mm (4in) guns and four 30mm CIWS, two depth-charge mortars and four 533mm (21in) torpedo tubes. Two Ka-27 Helix helicopters are also carried.

The Sovremenny class ships are similar in size but their main armament is eight SS-N-22 anti-ship missiles. No data are available for this very new weapon, but it is believed to have a range of up to 120km (75 miles) and probably has a nuclear warhead. Additional armament includes twin launchers for SA-N-7 anti-aircraft missiles, which have a range of 25km (16 miles), four 130mm (5in) guns and four 30mm CIWS, two mortars and four torpedo tubes for dual-purpose torpedoes.

US CRUISERS

The closest Western equivalents to these vessels are the American Ticonderoga and Virginia classes. The four vessels of the latter class were designed and built between 1976 and 1980 to supplement the two earlier California class guided missile cruisers built as nuclear-powered escorts for Nimitz class carriers. The Virginias are propelled by twin shafts driven by two D2G nuclear reactors which develop 60,000shp.

The Virginias, which appear strangely clean compared to the cluttered look of modern Soviet vessels, at first sight seem only to have single 127mm (5in) gun turrets fore and aft, but forward and aft of these are a pair of twin ASROC (anti-submarine rocket) belt-fed ver-

LEFT The most significant feature of the *Kirov* are the multiple hatches for the ship's many vertical-launch missile systems.

ABOVE LEFT Close-up of a Slava class vessel clearly shows the eight SS-N-12 launch tubes either side and the bow turret for two 133mm (5¹⁄₁₀in) guns.

ABOVE RIGHT The Soviet guided missile cruiser *Slava* in the Mediterranean.

RIGHT USS *Mississippi,* a Virginia class nuclear-powered guided missile cruiser, on patrol in the Atlantic.

LEFT Bow shot of USS *Ticonderoga* showing the box-like superstructure housing SPY-1 radar equipment.

BELOW RIGHT Aerial view of the USS *Ticonderoga*. Note the fore and aft 127mm (5in) gun turrets and twin SM-1 missile launchers, the satellite communications discs and the panels on the superstructure for the SPY-1 radar antennae.

tical launchers. This weapon, which is fitted to all major US surface warships other than carriers, is very similar to SUBROC: an RUR-5A missile with a range of 11.1km (6.9 miles) carries either a Mk 46 homing torpedo or a 1kT depth bomb to its target.

Unlike other more modern weapons systems – ASROC came into service in 1961 – the missile cannot have its guidance corrected in mid-flight despite the fact that the Virginia class carry what are known as LAMPS helicopters. The acronym stands for Light Airborne Multi-Purpose System and can be applied to any helicopter fitted for anti-submarine warfare and/or ASW missile guidance. Current LAMPS machines are the SH-2F Seasprite and SH-60B Seahawk. Because of ASROC's deficiencies in a modern war environment, the Virginia class cruisers are being retrofitted with Harpoon and Tomahawk as well as Phalanx CIWS. Other weaponry includes six 324mm

(12¾in) torpedo tubes for the standard USN Mk 46 lightweight torpedoes, which can also be carried by helicopter.

The Ticonderoga class cruisers have been designed to meet exactly the sort of threat posed by Soviet Kirov class battlecruisers which can launch a positive barrage of nuclear or conventional missiles. Their main armament is two twin Mk 26 Standard launchers

BELOW A SH-60B Seahawk LAMPS helicopter lands aboard a Virginia class cruiser.

(For full specifications of cruisers described, see page 126.)

INSET ABOVE Part of the Aegis control centre, heart of the Ticonderoga class's fighting system.

ABOVE A Phalanx installation aboard USS *Ticonderoga*. The bulbous white dome contains the gun's tracking radar.

OPPOSITE HMS *Broadsword*. The four Exocet launchers in the bow have been replaced in later vessels of the same class by eight Harpoons.

CRUISERS							
Cruiser Class	**Country of Origin**	**DIMENSIONS (M)**			**Displacement (tons)**	**Speed (knots)**	**Major weapons fit**
		Length	**Beam**	**Draught**			
Belknap	America	166.7	16.7	8.7	7,930	33	SM-1, ASROC, 1 × 127mm
Kara	Russia	174	18	6	9,500	32	SS-N-14, SS-N-4, 4 × 76mm
Kresta II	Russia	158	17	6	7,500	34	SS-N-14, SS-N-3, 4 × 57mm
Moskva	Russia	191	34	8	18,000	30	18 Ka-25, SA-N-3, 4 × 57mm

with 44 missiles apiece. The current SM-1 version of Standard is due to be replaced with the extended-range SM-2 at the end of the decade.

Standard SM-1 has been around since the 1960s; it is a conventional solid-fueled missile with a high-explosive warhead and a range of some 28km (17½ miles). SM-2 will have greater range and could carry a nuclear warhead as well. What is significant in the Ticonderoga class cruisers is the missiles' incorporation in the phenomenally expensive Aegis radar-controlled combat system.

Conventional radars can only scan one sector of the sky at a time so against an incoming wave of up to 20 Soviet missiles would be unable to cope with guiding an equal number of anti-missile missiles. In the Ticonderoga cruisers four SPY-1 radar arrays are installed on the superstructure: each covers a 45° arc, and each individual radar contains more than 4,000 detection elements constantly sweeping every inch of sky within that arc. Between them they are capable of directing up to 22 Standards against incoming missiles. It is intended that

two Ticonderoga class cruisers will ultimately be assigned to escort each Nimitz class carrier.

Because of the huge cost of the Aegis system, early plans to make the Ticonderogas nuclear-powered were shelved. Instead they have four gas turbines developing 80,000shp and driving twin shafts to give a top speed of 55km/h (30 knots). Additional armament includes Harpoon and Tomahawk, as well as the 127mm (5in) guns, a pair of Phalanx CIWS, ASROC and six 324mm (12¾in) torpedo tubes. Two LAMPS helicopters are carried in a hangar at the rear of the main superstructure.

Apart from obsolete or obsolescent warships sold to smaller navies, the only other classes of cruiser still serving are detailed in the accompanying table though several modern destroyers could be classed as cruisers because of their size.

DESTROYERS AND FRIGATES

The sheer number of destroyers and frigates, both of which types are today primarily designed as either anti-submarine weapon platforms or dedicated anti-aircraft vessels, precludes a detailed examination, so four ships are included as representative of modern designs. Destroyers and frigates are the workhorses of the fleet, and exist in far greater numbers than any other major warship classes. They are fast and versatile but, as shown in the Falklands, are very vulnerable to modern anti-ship missiles. This realization has led to many improvements in the use of fire-resistant materials and fire-fighting systems. However, naval architects had been aware of the hazards long before 1982 but it took a public and professional outcry at the losses to get anything done in the Royal Navy. What is perhaps most significant is that virtually every other nation has followed suit.

THE TYPE 22

The British Type 22 large frigates, batch 1 vessels being designated Broadsword, batch 2 as Boxer and batch 3 as Cornwall classes, have probably benefited most of all from the lessons of the Falklands, *Broadsword* herself and her sister *Brilliant* both having taken part in that campaign. Designed originally to replace the very successful Leander class frigates, which have themselves been subject to many modifications over the years, the Broadsword class

ABOVE A Westland Lynx of the Royal Navy armed with four Sea Skua anti-shipping missiles.

OPPOSITE An Exocet missile beneath the wing of a French Super Étendard strike aircraft. It was this aircraft/missile combination which sank HMS *Sheffield* and the *Atlantic Conveyor* in 1982.

should really be classed as destroyers rather than frigates.

Batch 2 vessels have a full load displacement of 5,090 tonnes (4,800 tons) but batch 3s displace 5,195 tonnes (4,900 tons) as a result of new and heavier armament. Gone are the four Exocet missile launchers and in their place have come a single 114mm (4½in) gun turret and eight Harpoon launchers. The 12 Seawolf anti-aircraft missile launchers are, however, retained. This extremely effective lightweight missile is so accurate that in trials it proved capable of shooting a 114mm (4½in) shell out of the air, and with a range of approximately 10km (6 miles) Seawolf can tackle both enemy aircraft and anti-ship missiles. An improved

vertically launched version, which does away with blind spots caused by the parent vessel's own superstructure, is being introduced.

For close-in defence against air attack the Type 22 batch 3s have the new Goalkeeper CIWS. This is a Dutch-designed seven-barrel Gatling-type weapon of 30mm calibre with a rate of fire of 4,200rds/min, both significant improvements over Phalanx. Other weapons include two Tigerfish torpedo tubes and Corvus and SRBOC chaff dispensers. In addition, two Lynx or Sea King helicopters are carried.

THE GEORGES LEYGUES CLASS

While the Type 22s are intended primarily for anti-submarine warfare, with a secondary anti-aircraft capability, the French Georges Leygues class actually includes two types of ship with a common hull, one for anti-submarine warfare and the other as a dedicated anti-aircraft platform; eight of the former and four of the latter vessels are planned at this time. These 4,420-tonne (4,170-ton) destroyers are powered by two gas turbines and two diesels which produce 52,000 and 10,400shp respectively.

The main anti-submarine armament installed on the Georges Leygues class is the 533mm (21in) L5 torpedo, for which two tubes are mounted. This torpedo has a speed of 65km/h (35 knots), which is inadequate to catch the latest Soviet submarines, and it will be replaced in due course. On the AA vessels the principal weapon will be the Crotale surface-to-air missile, 26 of which will be carried. This is a radar beam-guided missile with a range of 10km (6 miles), mid-course guidance corrections being given by the ship herself or by her Lynx helicopter. Other weapons common to both types are four Exocet launchers, a single 100mm (4in) gun and two 20mm light anti-aircraft guns.

Exocet is probably the best-known of all anti-ship missiles, though the version used by the Argentinians in the South Atlantic was the air-launched variant. It is a fire-and-forget missile which, once launched in the right direction, will employ its own active radar homing head to close with its target. A high subsonic missile, it has a range of more than 42km (26 miles) and a 165kg (360lb) warhead, and a supersonic version which will be even harder to detect and destroy is under development.

THE SPRUANCE CLASS

The largest of all modern destroyers are those of the American Spruance class. Designed from the outset to be very spacious and easily modified to accept new weapon systems and sensors as they were developed, so as to prolong hull life, the Spruances are ungainly, boxlike vessels but very effective for all that. There are 32 in service plus four Kidd class vessels which were originally built for export to Iran but withheld when the Shah was deposed. The Kidds have a primary anti-aircraft role whereas the original vessels are mainly ASW platforms. The Spruances are powered by four gas turbines generating 80,000shp through twin shafts.

Main armament of the Spruance class comprises two quadruple Harpoon launchers, one eight-barrel Sea Sparrow surface-to-air missile launcher (the Kidds have two), two 127mm (5in) guns, two Phalanx CIWS, an ASROC launcher and two triple torpedo tubes. The vessels also carry two LAMPS helicopters and will be retrofitted with Tomahawk cruise missiles.

ABOVE The fire-control antennae for the Sea Sparrow SAMs aboard a Spruance class warship.

SOVIET DESTROYERS

The Soviet Navy has no true modern destroyer, though several of the Kashin class built in the 1960s continue in service. They are mainly significant in that they pioneered gas turbine propulsion, since copied in many Western warships. The Kashin class was superseded in production by the much smaller Krivak class, which also use gas turbine propulsion, 72,000shp through two shafts giving them a maximum speed of 59km/h (32 knots).

Vessels of the original version, designated Krivak I, have two twin 76mm (3in) gun turrets while the later Krivak IIs have two single 100mm (4in) turrets. Otherwise the armament is the same for both: four large SS-N-14 anti-ship missile launchers in the bow, two twin SA-N-4 anti-aircraft missile launchers with 40 reloads, two depth-charge mortars and eight 533mm (21in) torpedo tubes. A further development, designated Krivak III, has two 30mm CIWS in place of one of the SA-N-4 launchers.

Details of a selection of other destroyers and frigates in current service are given in the accompanying table.

LEFT The bow 127mm (5in) gun turret on the USS *Elliot*.

BELOW LEFT USS *Elliot*, a Spruance class destroyer designed primarily for anti-submarine warfare.

DESTROYERS AND FRIGATES

Destroyer Frigate	Country of Origin	Length	Beam	Draught	Displacement (tons)	Speed (knots)	Main weapons
Amazon	Britain	117	12.3	5.8	3,250	30	1 × 114mm, 4 × Exocet, 1 × 4 Seacat SAM, 6 × 533mm tubes
Georges Leygues	France	139.0	14.0	5.7	4,170	30	1 × 100mm, 2 × 533mm tubes, Exocet
Godavari	India	121	14.1	9	3,600	27	4 × SS-N-2, 1 × SA-N-4, 2 × 2 57mm, 6 × tubes
Iroquois	America	129.8	15.2	4.4	4,700	29	1 × 127mm, 2 × Sea Sparrow, 2 × tubes
Kashin	Russia	143.0	16.0	5.0	4,500	35	SA-N-1, mortars, 4 × 76mm, 5 × 533mm tubes
Kortenaer	Holland	130	14.4	4.4	3,630	30	1 × 4 Harpoon, 1 × 8 Sea Sparrow, 2 × 76mm, 2 × tubes
Krivak	Russia	123.0	14.0	5.0	3,600	30	SS-N-14, SA-N-4, 2 × 2 76mm or 2 × 1 100mm, mortars, 8 × 533mm tubes
Luda	China	131	13.7	4.6	3,900	36	6 × SSM, 2 × ASW launchers, 2 × 2 133mm
Oliver Hazard Perry	America	135.6	13.7	4.5	3,605	29	1 × Harpoon, 1 × 76mm, 1 × Phalanx, 2 × tubes
Spruance	America	171.7	16.8	5.8	7,810	33	Harpoon, Sea Sparrow, 2 × 127mm, ASROC, 6 × 533mm tubes
Type 22 Broadsword Batch 1	Britain	131.2	14.75	4.3	4,200	30	Seawolf, Exocet, Corvus, STWS
Batch 2	Britain	143.6	14.75	6.4	4,800	30	Seawolf, Exocet, Corvus, STWS
Batch 3	Britain	143.6	14.75	6.4	4,900	30	1 × 114mm, Seawolf, Harpoon, Corvus, SRBOC, STWS-2

3

FIREPOWER
IN THE AIR

modern strike aircraft such as the Panavia Tornado can carry more destructive power under its sleek wings than could be borne by an armada of World War II Lancasters or Flying Fortresses. With sophisticated terrain-following radar, the ability to fly hundreds of miles day or night at high transonic speeds and at rooftop heights, with sophisticated electronic and physical countermeasures gear to put off enemy fighters and missiles, such aircraft are highly capable and equipped to survive a nuclear or conventional conflict – once they are in the air, of course. They are also vastly complex, hugely expensive, and training their crews alone costs the earth.

To combat them the traditional short-range high-speed interceptor has given way to the so-called air superiority fighter. Characterized by greater endurance, look-up, look-down and sideways scan radar and fire-and-forget missiles, the latter are capable of locking on to and shooting down enemy aircraft over dozens of miles – under the right conditions, at least, for a weaving aircraft partially hidden from radar in the ground clutter and obscured from infra-red by cloud or rain is an elusive target at best. The penalty for such sophisticated systems, epitomized by the American F-15 Eagle, is again their enormous cost so the lightweight fighter has gained appreciable popularity over recent years, especially in smaller countries with budgets more limited than those of the superpowers.

AIRFIELD VULNERABILITY

The main problem with all the above types of aircraft is that they spend most of their time on the ground, on large vulnerable airfields whose exact latitude and longitude are programmed into enemy missiles. According to aviation author Bill Gunston the Soviet Union has no fewer than 14 nuclear missiles permanently aimed at every airfield in the United States and Western Europe. Despite the presence of hardened aircraft shelters, which are only designed to protect against blast and fragmentation effects, no airfield is going to survive an all-out attack for longer than a few minutes into a war.

And where are those aircraft fortunate enough to take off in time going to land when they have completed their missions? Only the Swedes have devoted much thought to this

crucial problem, and their multi-role Saab Viggen aircraft regularly practise landing on and taking off from stretches of motorway miles away from any major targets. Maintenance trucks, fuel bowsers and trucks containing fresh supplies of bombs and missiles would be similarly dispersed in the event of an attack.

In crowded Western Europe, though, this can only be a partial answer; on the other hand, the British Aerospace Harrier provides a viable alternative. Able to operate from unprepared sites in the middle of forests, fields or even town centres, in time of war they would be dispersed all over the landscape. It has taken a long time for Sir Sidney Camm's team's brilliant concept to gain recognition and there are

TOP A Tornado photographed at Farnborough showing the bewildering array of armament which can be carried – though not all at once, of course!

ABOVE Although photographed here on the perimeter track of an airfield in Germany, the Harrier can operate equally effectively off small country roads in the middle of forests – or virtually anywhere else, come to that!

OPPOSITE A prototype Tornado F 2 ADV armed with four Sky Flash air-to-air missiles.

ABOVE A Tornado GR 1 photographed during a low-level exercise, armed with eight 454kg bombs, two drop tanks and two ECM/chaff pods.

still far too few Harriers in service, for after a couple of hours of a global war they would be about the only NATO fixed-wing aircraft surviving.

Helicopters, of course, share the Harriers' ability to land and take off from virtually anywhere, with the result that a wide variety of dedicated tank-busting and anti-submarine types are now in service. Even so, both helicopters and Harriers have only limited

endurance and weapons-lifting ability.

Supporting the above types are a large assortment of others, including in-flight refueling tankers and electronic warfare, airborne early warning (AEW) and airborne warning and control systems (AWACS) aircraft. However, the AEW and AWACS types need to fly at high altitudes and emit a great deal of noise throughout the infra-red and electronic spectra, so they are obvious and easy targets. Even

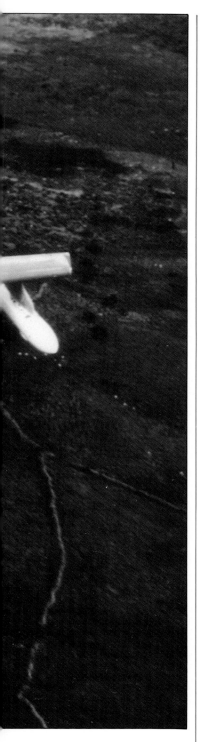

though they may have the ability to stay airborne for two or three days at a time, would they get the chance? Such questions, of course, postulate the worst of all possible cases – a global nuclear war – and modern military aircraft are still essential in the limited conflicts which have characterized post-1945 warfare from Korea to the Lebanon, and from Suez to the Falklands.

STRIKE AIRCRAFT

Several hundred Tornados are in service with the Royal Air Force, the West German Navy and Air Force and the Italian Air Force. By far the most important single military aircraft in Western Europe, it first entered service in 1980 with the Tornado Trinational Training Establishment at RAF Cottesmore, in England.

Tornado is a large and very impressive two-seat swing-wing all-weather attack aircraft, the fastest in the world at low levels and capable of carrying a greater weapons load over a longer range than any comparable type. One of its most important attributes is the on-board navigational computer operated, along with the ECM gear, by the back-seater. The flight plan is programmed into a master computer buried in the airfield's underground operations room, a very simple process taking next to no time. This computer produces a cassette which is simply inserted into the on-board computer: the computer does the rest, in conjunction with a terrain-following radar.

The Tornado has an integral armament of two 27mm Mauser cannon and can carry a wide variety of ordnance on seven fuselage and wing pylons. (Despite the fact that guns were considered obsolete 20 and more years ago, subsequent experience – not least that of the Israelis in their various wars – has proven that there is no substitute in aerial combat for the gun.)

TORNADO'S WEAPONS

However, the basic Tornado is not specifically designed for dogfighting and its most significant armament is its external payload. It is worth examining this in some detail as it is typical of the armament carried by all modern strike aircraft.

For use against enemy aircraft the main weapon is the AIM-9 Sidewinder in different variants. Developed in the USA in the early 1950s, this is the most influential air-to-air missile in the West, tens of thousands having been manufactured over the years for a wide variety of customers. Although now in need of replacement, it is still deployed in enormous numbers and remains a formidable weapon. A relatively small solid-fueled missile with a warhead of between 4.5kg and 11.4kg (10-25lb) depending on variant, in its most up-to-date form it has a combination laser/infra-red proximity fuze and a range of up to 19.3km (12 miles). This classifies it in the modern battlefield environment as a close-range weapon.

Sidewinder is due to be replaced throughout NATO in the early 1990s by ASRAAM (Advanced Short-Range Air-to-Air Missile), a joint development by Britain and West Germany which will have an advanced solid-fuel motor, a range in the region of 15km (9 miles) and a warhead of approximately 5kg (11lb). The major improvements over Sidewinder will probably lie in its homing system, which will make it a hittile. ASRAAM has been specifically designed to fit existing Sidewinder pylons without modification, which some critics say is a case of the tail wagging the dog. Certainly it could have been made more effective if this limitation had not applied.

Tornado can also carry ALARM (Air-Launched Anti-Radiation Missile), Sea Eagle, Kormoran and Maverick, with Harpoon a possibility for the future. ALARM is a British missile with a German warhead designed specifically to home on and destroy enemy radar installations; due to enter service alongside ASRAAM in the early 1990s, it is a two-stage solid-fueled missile with a range of some 10km (6 miles). Four passive multi-band radar receivers in the nose guide it unerringly to its target even through rapid wavelength changes. As well as ground installations, it can obviously be used against warships (though its small warhead would prevent much damage being done other than to the radar antennas) and against airborne early warning aircraft. As noted in the introduction, the only defence against such missiles is to shut down the broadcasting radar.

Sea Eagle, another new weapon, is a British-designed medium-range – approximately 30km (19 miles) – supersonic sea-skimming anti-ship missile. Warhead size is undisclosed but said to be of high lethality. Kormoran, the German equivalent, is a high subsonic two-stage solid-fueled missile which skims the sea at 30m (100ft) altitude and has a range of 37km (23 miles). It uses both active and passive radar to lock on but can also be fired optically. Its large 160kg (350lb) warhead is designed to penetrate up to 90mm (3½in) of steel plate before exploding, 16 radially-mounted charges being capable of penetrating seven of a ship's bulkheads.

Maverick is an American infra-red guided anti-tank missile which homes on the heat from a tank's engine. It normally has a 210kg (460lb) shaped-charge warhead easily capable of defeating any known armour. It is supersonic and has a range of up to 40km (25 miles) when launched at high altitude, though it would more normally be fired from close to ground level when range is 16km (10 miles). Target acquisition is made through a television sight but once released the missile is self-homing. A planned new version will even dispense with the need for the pilot to see the target first.

BOMBS, DISPENSERS AND CLUSTER BOMBS

Tornado can also carry conventional bombs, typically four 454kg (1,000lb) bombs which may be high explosive or the Type WE177 nuclear device of undisclosed yield. These are usually fitted with retarding fins or small parachutes to delay the rate of descent: otherwise there would be a real danger of such a low-flying aircraft blowing itself up.

Other munitions include the JP233 low-altitude airfield attack system and the BL755 cluster bomb. The former seems a rather pointless device since, as we have seen, in a time of all-out war it is unlikely that any airfields would survive. However, Britain is not alone in manufacturing such weapons, which seem to many people to be a case of armaments industries effectively conning the armed forces: the USA has the BLU-67, France the BAP 100 and Durandal, Spain the BRFA 330, Russia the BETAB, West Germany has MIFF, and so on. All are similar in design and purpose, comprising a large number of relatively small sub-munitions, released from a dispenser beneath an aircraft, whose prime purpose is to crater airfield runways, making them unusable. The

cratering bomblets themselves are usually accompanied by anti-personnel mines, delivered in the same package, to endanger the crews repairing damaged runways.

Other cluster bombs, as such weapons are generally known, are more sensible, being designed to attack enemy armoured fighting vehicles from above, where their armour is generally thinnest. The British BL755, for example, carries 147 bomblets in seven bays in the dispenser; the bomblets are designed to fall at different speeds so as to spread themselves as widely as possible over the battlefield. They are stabilized in flight by sprung steel tails which ensure they fall vertically so that when they hit a tank the shaped-charge warhead will achieve maximum penetration – in the case of the BL755 said to be at least 250mm (10in) of armour plate. These unpleasant little devices also shatter sideways when they hit, up to 2,000 metal fragments flying outwards to kill or cripple any exposed infantrymen who may be in the vicinity. Delayed-action systems are also available, in which the bomblets are effectively dual-purpose anti-armour and anti-personnel mines.

A recent American development along these lines is the self-forging fragment, which will be more effective against reactive armour, an Israeli invention now being widely copied. Reactive armour consists of small tiles, rather like those on the Space Shuttle but composed of an explosive compound. They are bolted to the armour plating of a tank and when hit by a shaped-charge shell, bomb or missile they explode outwards, dissipating and nullifying the stream of molten plasma which would otherwise penetrate the armour. They cannot be detonated by accident – for example, by small arms fire – and do not react to each other, so that if one is set off it does not detonate adjacent tiles. The Israelis rather appropriately call this system Blazer.

The self-forging fragment is rather more difficult to explain. Otherwise known as an explosively-formed projectile, its basis is a lens of metal coupled to a micro-processor detector and an explosive charge. The device can be dropped from an aircraft, fired from a gun or incorporated in a missile warhead. Over its target – typically a group of tanks – the micro-processor steers the projectile by means of vanes or parachutes and detects when it is at the

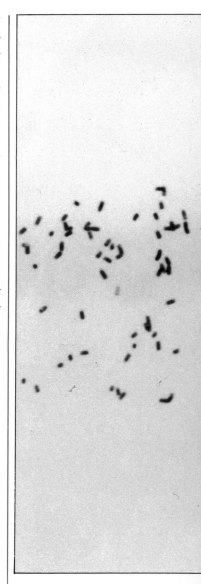

RIGHT A Tornado of the West German Navy carrying four Kormoran anti-shipping missiles.

ABOVE A West German Navy Tornado liberally distributes MIFF anti-personnel mines from its MW-1 multiple dispenser.

correct distance. At this point the explosive charge detonates, compressing and re-forming the metal lens into a pointed, solid armour-piercing projectile and imparting an enormous velocity to it. This is enough to penetrate the upper armour of any known tank, and the projectile is not deterred by reactive armour.

Six or more such submunitions can be carried in a container the approximate size of a 500kg (1,000lb) bomb or 155mm (6in) artillery shell. If the inbuilt guidance system fails to detect a suitable target during the descent, the weapon turns itself into a mine upon landing, ready to launch itself upward against the relatively soft belly armour of a tank or other AFV. The American system is called Skeet and represents the latest state-of-the-art technology in smart ordnance – that is, munitions that find their own target after they have been launched.

THE PHANTOM

Other strike aircraft sharing similar attributes to Tornado include the elderly Phantom, probably the best-known Western combat aircraft of the post-1945 era and despite its age – the first prototype flew in 1958 – still a potent weapons platform. More than 5,000 have been built, making it the most widely used strike aircraft in the West.

The variants are far too numerous to describe in any detail, but the E version, which is the most widely used, is powered by two afterburning General Electric turbojets which generate 8,120kg (17,900lb) of thrust to give it a top speed of Mach 2.27 at high altitudes. Normal armament comprises four AIM-7 Sparrow air-to-air missiles under the fuselage and either two further Sparrows or four Sidewinders under the wings in addition to the integral 20mm Gatling-type gun.

Sparrow is another elderly missile due to be replaced by AMRAAM. (Advanced Medium-Range Air-to-Air Missile). It first entered service with the US Air Force in 1956 and is currently used by ten other nationalities, including the RAF. The most recent AIM-7F variant has solid-state guidance circuitry which gives room for a more powerful fragmentation warhead than in earlier marks. Its solid-fuel rocket motor gives it a top speed of Mach 4 and a range of 100km (62 miles). It has both proximity and impact fuzes and the warhead is encased in a continuous rod of stainless steel which fragments into 2,600 pieces.

The Phantom can also carry a wide variety of air-to-ground ordnance including free-fall bombs, napalm canisters, the Maverick anti-tank missile and Shrike or HARM anti-radiation missiles. Shrike, a development of Sparrow, was the first pure anti-radiation missile in the world, entering service in 1963 and seeing action in Vietnam and, in Israeli hands, in the Middle East. It has a range of up to 40km (25 miles) depending on the aircraft's height at launch and a powerful 66kg (145lb) warhead.

HARM – High-speed Anti-Radiation Missile – was developed in the early 1970s as a replacement and began entering service in 1983. While shorter-ranged than Shrike, it travels at much higher velocity, reducing time to target and therefore giving the enemy radar operators less time to react. Range is actually 16km (10 miles);

BELOW A Phantom FGR 2 of the famous 111 ('Treble One') Squadron.

RIGHT A pair of F-15s of the USAF each carrying four Sparrows and Sidewinders as well as ECM pods. The 20mm gun in the nose is very prominent.

the warhead is a proximity-fuzed fragmentation type of undisclosed weight.

THE F-111

The big, swing-swing General Dynamics F-111 was, until the introduction of Tornado, the world's best long-range all-weather strike aircraft despite the enormous political and financial problems before it entered service in 1967. Like Tornado, it is a two-seater, though in this case the crewmen sit side by side instead of in tandem. The most important variants are the F-111F, a tactical attack aircraft carrying conventional weapons, and the FB-111A, the nuclear strike version which serves alongside the B-52 and B-1B in Strategic Air Command. Both versions have large internal bomb bays and six underwing pylons which, as on the Tornado, swivel automatically as the wings are extended or retracted.

The FB-111A can carry up to six 1MT B43 or B61 nuclear bombs, the latter having a yield

of anything from 10kT to 500kT depending on the assigned target. These can be fuzed for air or ground burst and may be parachute-retarded to give the delivery aircraft more time to make its escape. The aircraft can also carry as an alternative six AGM-69A SRAMs (Short Range Attack Missiles), two internally and four under the wings. This supersonic solid-fuel missile has a range of up to 169km (105 miles) and carries a 200kT warhead.

A new 1MT bomb designated B83 will form part of future payloads for FB-111As. This has been designed to be dropped at supersonic speeds from altitudes of less than 50m (165ft) and still allow the delivery aircraft to escape. It is specifically designed to knock out hardened missile silos and presumably buries itself deeply before exploding as well as having variable delayed action fuzing and/or parachute retardation.

The F-111F is now equipped with the Pave Tack targeting pod, which is carried in the internal bay but rotated out on a cradle for use. The most important thing about the pod when used in conjunction with smart weapons is its extremely accurate laser target marker.

THE JAGUAR

Although produced in relatively small numbers, the Anglo-French SEPECAT Jaguar single-seat strike aircraft is an important tactical weapon. As with the RAF's Harriers, one of its most important features is the laser nose which enables the pilot to be guided to a target he cannot see by laser markers deployed by ground forces or helicopters. This gives great accuracy even in conditions of poor visibility. The Jaguar is armed with two 30mm French DEFA or British Aden cannon and a typical stores load would comprise centreline fuel tank with two laser-guided bombs, an ECM pod and a chaff dispenser or Martel anti-shipping missiles beneath the wings; it can also carry Sidewinder or Magic air-to-air missiles on overwing pylons.

Martel exists in two versions, one radar-seeking and the other controlled by means of a television camera in its nose. The radar-guided variant is principally used by the French Air Force as an anti-radiation weapon, while the TV version used by the RAF is being replaced by Sea Eagle. Although now outdated, Martel

OPPOSITE An F-111 dropping a cluster of 'slick' low-drag bombs on its target. In inter-service bombing competitions, the aircraft comes a sad second to the Tornado.

ABOVE F-111F with Pave Tack laser target designator and four laser-guided bombs.

LEFT Loading up a Jaguar with 454kg (1,000lb) bombs.

BELOW A Jaguar GR 1 of the RAF with a centreline drop tank, two laser-guided bombs, an ECM pod on the port outer pylon and a chaff dispenser under the starboard wing.

is a powerful weapon with a 150kg (330lb) warhead and an estimated range of 60km (37 miles). Magic is a French snap-fire infra-red-guided AAM, solid-fueled and with a range of 10km (6 miles). It has only a small 12.5kg (28lb) high-explosive fragmentation warhead but is very accurate and highly manoeuvrable, being able to stand acceleration forces of 50g. The missile's biggest drawback is that its rocket motor emits vast clouds of smoke, giving extra visual warning to an enemy pilot and helping him evade it. It is due to be replaced in the 1990s by MICA, which will be even more manoeuvrable and have a range of some 50km (30 miles).

THE VIGGEN

The Swedish Viggen, one of the most impressive combat aircraft in service anywhere, exists in five main variants. The most important is the AJ37 single-seat all-weather strike fighter, which is equally at home attacking targets on the ground or at sea. Visually, the single most striking feature of the Viggen is its canard fore-

planes. These give the aircraft extraordinary manoeuvrability and will be a feature of the new JAS39 Gripen which will eventually replace the Viggen.

In its fighter/interceptor version Viggen powers to 10,000m (33,000ft) in 100 seconds from starting its take-off run, a performance only excelled by more modern types such as the F-15 Eagle. In addition to its 30mm Oerlikon cannon, the Viggen can carry a wide

TOP AND ABOVE whether in its attack (camouflaged) or interceptor version, the Swedish Saab Viggen is one of the most impressive and capable of all modern fighter aircraft. Its ability to take off from and land on relatively short stretches of road rather than properly prepared runways gives it greatly enhanced survivability.

81

range of weapons on seven underwing pylons including free-fall bombs to anti-tank, anti-ship and air-to-air missiles. It has a tactical radius of over 1,000km (620 miles) with external drop tanks and, as noted earlier, the ability to operate from relatively short stretches of motorway.

SOVIET STRIKE AIRCRAFT

The Soviet Union's principal tactical strike aircraft are the Sukhoi Su-17/-20/-22 Fitter and Su-24 Fencer. (Su-20 and Su-22 are designations for export versions of the -17.) Both are swing-wing machines but only the more modern Su-24 has genuine all-weather capability. The Su-17 first appeared to Western observers in 1967; typical weapons include Atoll or Aphid air-to-air missiles for self-defence, PTAB anti-tank cluster bomb dispensers and free-fall conventional or nuclear bombs. (There are more than a thousand different types of Russian aerial bomb, ranging in weight from 100kg to 1,000kg [220-2,200lb], including 14 nuclear weapons of differing yields, so it is impossible to enumerate them all here.) The aircraft also has twin 30mm cannon.

It is possible that the Su-17 may also carry AS-7 Kerry tactical air-to-surface missiles. Known to be a major weapons fit for the Su-24, Kerry is a transonic missile with a 100kg (220lb) warhead and a range of about 11km (7 miles); it is due to be replaced by the AS-10 Karen laser-guided version. The AS-8, air-

launched version of the AT-6 Spiral anti-tank missile discussed in the next chapter, is another possibility.

The Su-24 Fencer is a twin-engined, two-seat strike aircraft bearing a marked resemblance to the Tornado, although it has side-by-side seating like the F-111. Indeed, it is believed that it was developed almost as a direct copy of the latter aircraft. Very few details have ever been made available, but the aircraft has eight hardpoints for underwing stores. These can include the weapons mentioned above as well as the AS-X-9 anti-radiation missile, about which no data are available except that range is believed to be circa 88km (55 miles), and nuclear bombs. It is certain that the Su-24 has Doppler and terrain-following radars, a laser target seeker and electronic countermeasures equipment. More than 800 are in service, making it one of the most important aircraft in the Warsaw Pact inventory.

BELOW Sukhoi Su-24 with fuselage-mounted drop tanks which give it its formidable range. A variety of EW/ECM antennae and fairings can be seen on the tail and around the nose.

BOTTOM The beautiful lines of the F/A-18A Hornet are no more decorative than were those of the wartime Spitfire, but designed to make it as easy to fly as possible so that the pilot can concentrate upon the enemy.

RIGHT Grumman EA-6B Prowlers in formation – something which would not be seen in time of war.

BELOW RIGHT The supremely powerful and versatile F-14 Tomcat, seen here armed with four under-fuselage Phoenix missiles and a single Sparrow and Sidewinder under each wing for closer-range use.

THE F-14 TOMCAT

One specialized type of strike aircraft is the naval attack aircraft. In this category the most powerful by far is the US Navy's F-14 Tomcat, though there are also numerous British Buccaneers, French Super Étendards and American Intruders, Skyhawks and Corsairs around, to name just the principal types.

The F-14, as mentioned in the previous chapter, is deployed aboard the Nimitz class nuclear-powered fleet carriers. A two-seat multi-role fighter, the Tomcat is big, immensely powerful and highly manoeuvrable, thanks to automatic compensators which adjust the wing angle to the optimum configuration for what the pilot is trying to do, without his having to think about it. More than 500 are in service with 24 US Navy squadrons as well as with Iran; the Iranian aircraft were supplied before

the coup which overthrew the Shah and they have seen extensive – and apparently successful – combat in the continuing Gulf War with Iraq.

The Tomcat has a single M61 Vulcan cannon and can carry a wide range of ordnance under the fuselage and wings, including four Sparrows plus up to eight Sidewinders or four AIM-54 Phoenix plus two Sidewinders. The F-14 is the only aircraft tasked to carry Phoenix. This big, long-range missile costs more than a million dollars a time and has the largest active/passive radar scanner in any air-to-air missile in the world, backed up by an infra-red homing system. The aircraft/missile weapon system is so flexible that up to six independent targets can be tracked and attacked simultaneously, and in tests against target drones employing electronic countermeasures, four hits out of six, with one mis-fire, have been achieved. Phoenix is powered by a long-burning solid fuel motor which gives it a speed of Mach 5+ and the missile has exceptional manoeuvrability to enable it to hit its target despite evasive tactics. It has proximity, infra-red and impact fuzing.

THE F/A-18 HORNET

The McDonnell Douglas F/A-18 Hornet was originally planned to be a less expensive successor to the F-14: even so, it ended up

costing over $20 million a copy. Nevertheless, the Hornet is being purchased by Australia, Canada and Spain.

The F/A-18 is a compromise aircraft in several respects and, although a superb combat machine by any standards, lacks both the F-14's endurance and manoeuvrability in the fighter role and the Tornado's terrain-following ability in the low-level attack configuration. The weapons fit can include the Harpoon anti-ship missile, Sparrows, Sidewinders, bombs, ECM pods, and so on, up to a maximum of 6,080kg (13,400lb) for a catapult takeoff from a carrier. The aircraft also has a single M61 Vulcan cannon.

OTHER NAVAL STRIKE AIRCRAFT

Although the Hornet in US Navy and Marine Corps service will eventually replace both the F-4 Phantom and the Vought A-7 Corsair, the latter is still an important naval attack aircraft.

The same is true of the A-6 Intruder and EA-6 Prowler which will continue in produc-

BELOW Dassault Breguet Super Étendards overfly a fleet of small pleasure boats in a delicious peacetime Riviera setting. War would be rather different again.

ABOVE **ABOVE** F-15 Eagle armed with four Sparrow and two Sidewinder air-to-air missiles.

tion for the foreseeable future.

In a rather different category, although still a maritime strike aircraft, the Lockheed S-3 Viking is a dedicated anti-submarine platform. A four-man crew is necessary to operate the complex computer, radar, sonobuoy and magnetic anomaly detector gear as well as fly it and operate the weapon systems. Its weapons load comprises Harpoon, rocket pods, cluster or conventional bombs and mines on external pylons plus four air-launched torpedoes, bombs, mines or depth bombs in the internal weapons bay.

The Soviet Union has no comparable carrier-based aircraft as yet, relying on the Flogger (described later) and long-range land-based maritime patrol aircraft. Nor has the Royal Navy since *Ark Royal* was scrapped and its Buccaneers were handed over to the RAF where they soldier on alongside the Tornados and Phantoms.

Only France has persevered with the dedicated carrier-borne strike aircraft in the shape of the Dassault-Breguet Super Étendard. Although now an elderly aircraft and due to be replaced when the first French nuclear carrier, *Charles de Gaulle,* enters service at the turn of the century, the Super Étendard is still a very effective weapons platform. Iraqi aircraft have sunk or damaged several ships in the Persian Gulf, and Argentinian Super Étendards were responsible for the loss of HMS *Sheffield* and the *Atlantic Conveyor* in the South Atlantic. In addition to Exocet, whose attributes are well known since the Falklands, the aircraft has two 30mm DEFA cannons.

AIR SUPERIORITY FIGHTERS

The broad function of air superiority fighters is the same as that of the interceptors they have largely replaced: to shoot down enemy aircraft. The classic example of this type is the McDonnell Douglas F-15 Eagle, a single-seat, twin-engine aircraft which bears a superficial resemblance to the Tomcat. However, it is

NAVAL STRIKE AIRCRAFT									
Aircraft name	Length	DIMENSIONS (M) Height	Span	Loaded weight (kg)	Engine(s)	Max speed (km/h)	Max range (km)	Max ceiling (m)	Main weapons carried
BAe Buccaneer	19.33	4.95	13.41	27,123	2 × RR 5,003kg turbofans	1,110	3,700	15,000	Sea Eagle, Martel, bombs, rockets
Dassault-Breguet Super Etendard	14.31	3.85	9.6	11,500	1 × SNECMA 5,110kg turbojet	1,200 (sea level)	650 (combat radius)	13,700+	Exocet, 2 × 30mm, bombs
Grumman F-14 Tomcat	19.1	4.88	11.63 to 19.54	32,658	2 × P&W or GE 9,480 or 13,154kg turbofans	2,157 (high), 1,470 (sea level)	3,200	17,070+	Phoenix, AIM-9, AIM-7, 1 × M61 Vulcan
McDonnell Douglas F/A-18 Hornet	17.07	4.66	11.42	22,317	2 × GE 7,258kg turbofans	1,915 (high)	741 (combat radius)	15,000+	Harpoon, AIM-9, AIM-7, bombs, 1 × M61 Vulcan

*Note: The Phantom is still very much a naval strike aircraft as well in the US Navy and elsewhere; see earlier for details.

actually a very different aircraft, not least because it has fixed rather than variable-geometry wings.

The Eagle, which entered service in 1974, was the result of a USAF requirement in the mid-1960s for a new aircraft to replace existing machines such as the F-100, F-102, F-104 and F-106. It was designed to have the longest possible endurance, which is usually equated with range but actually means an aircraft's ability to stay in the air for as long as possible. This is obviously important for a fighter which will need to intercept incoming aircraft as far as possible from their intended target and engage them in combat for as long as possible before landing to refuel and re-arm. However, the US Department of Defense is naturally reluctant to release endurance figures for the F-15 so we have to be satisfied with partial figures for range, which really mean little in this context, though a ferry range of 4,630km (2,875 miles) with three drop tanks suggests that its endurance must be pretty good.

Current armament of the Eagle is four Sparrows and four Sidewinders, but these will be replaced by AMRAAM and ASRAAM. (The US Air Force experimented with the Navy's Phoenix missile but has not adopted it.) The aircraft's avionics give it excellent manoeuvrability in a dogfight and a highly sophisticated look-down radar enables it to track and engage low-flying strike aircraft or cruise missiles. The new F-15E two-seat strike aircraft will have additional Doppler and terrain-following radars operated by the back-seater. It will carry up to 11,113kg (24,500lb) of external stores, including both bombs and air-to-surface missiles.

The British equivalent of the Eagle is the Tornado F3 ADV (Air Defence Variant) which has just started entering service. Differences between it and the standard strike version include automatic sweep control for greater manoeuvrability and the Foxhunter look-up/look-down radar to enable it to track several different targets at high or low levels up to 185km (115 miles) away. The Tornado ADV has an endurance of 2hr 20min flying time 600km (370 miles) from its base. Its four Sky Flash missiles (to be replaced by ASRAAM), based on the American Sparrow but with British electronics, are solid-fueled supersonic missiles with a range of 40km (25 miles) and a 30kg (66lb) warhead.

BELOW A MiG-23 of the Soviet Air Force during a goodwill visit to Finland.

SOVIET FIGHTERS

The latest Soviet multi-role aircraft are the MiG-29 Fulcrum, MiG-31 Foxhound and Su-27 Flanker, which will eventually supplement and replace the earlier MiG-23 and MiG-27, themselves already extremely advanced and capable machines. The MiG-23 and -27 are essentially the same aircraft, the former tasked for the air superiority role and the latter for strike duties, just as in the case of Tornado. A single-seat, single-engine, swing-wing design, it has a tall reinforced undercarriage to allow it to operate from rough or unprepared airstrips.

A wide variety of ordnance can be carried. The MiG-23 has a single 23mm GSh-23 gun and hardpoints for two AA-7 Apex and four AA-8 Aphid anti-aircraft missiles. Both are solid-fueled rockets: Apex, the larger, is designed for use at ranges up to 35km (22 miles) and exists in two different versions, one with radar and the other with infra-red homing, both sharing the same 40kg (88lb) warhead. The much smaller Aphid is designed for close-in dogfighting, with a range of only 5km (3 miles) and a warhead of about 8kg (18lb). Sharing several features with the French Magic missile, it is extremely manoeuvrable. The MiG-27 can carry up to 16 250kg (550lb) FAB bombs under the fuselage and six 100kg (220lb) FABs under the wings, as well as cluster dispensers, two AS-7 Kerry or AS-10 Karen missiles or – an unusual configuration these days – two underwing GSh-23 gun pods angled downward so the aircraft can attack a target while remaining in level flight. The GSh-23's rate of fire is 3,000rds/min.

The MiG-25 Foxbat has probably been the best-known Soviet fighter ever since Victor Belenko defected to Japan in his aircraft, allowing Western experts to examine one at first-hand. Having superficial similarities with the F-15, it is a large fixed-wing, single-seat, twin-engined and twin-tailed air superiority aircraft. Weapons carried are as for the MiG-23 with the addition of the AA-6 Acrid long-range (80km [50 miles]) solid-fueled missile, which has a large 90kg (200lb) warhead and can be radar-guided or infra-red homing.

The MiG-29 is smaller than the Foxbat and lacks its brute power but is far more sophisticated, having advanced avionics comparable to those of the F-15 for enhanced manoeuvrability

at all heights and, for the first time in a modern Soviet fighter, a high-placed bubble canopy to give the pilot decent all-round vision. (Pilots of earlier types have a very restricted rearward view.) Few details are available, but it carries the AA-10 Alamo, a new air-to-air missile with an estimated range of 30km (19 miles).

The MiG-31 Foxhound is a big, long-range interceptor loosely based on the MiG-25 but with a revised cockpit and semi-bubble canopy similar to that on the Tornado to accommodate a second crew member. Its radar and ECM, comparable to anything in the West, allow it to engage multiple targets at all heights with its eight AA-9 Amos missiles. Amos, another new air-to-air weapon, is believed to be on a par with the US Navy's Phoenix, having a range of some 130km (80 miles) and a warhead weighing around 80kg (175lb) which could be either conventional or nuclear. It is a fire-and-forget missile which automatically seeks its target once launched.

The Sukhoi Su-27 is, in general terms, a scaled-up MiG-29 and has been specifically designed to be able to outfly the latest Western fighters and strike aircraft. Indeed, the Soviets are past masters at letting Western designers and engineers sort the bugs out of a system at huge cost and then copying it themselves. From the MiG-29 onward all Soviet combat aircraft have incorporated features copied from the latest American designs.

With the hard work done for them it is relatively easy for Soviet designers to go one stage further, and that is what has happened with the Su-27. With a sophisticated multi-mode pulse-Doppler radar it can track several targets; it carries eight AA-10 missiles.

TOP On the ground, the resemblance between this MiG-29 and the F-15 is very striking.

ABOVE The close resemblance of the MiG-29 to the F-15 is clearly apparent here. The aircraft carries a variety of AAMs and ECM pods.

LEFT Close-up of a MiG-23 armed with AA-2 Atoll AAMs which are now being replaced by AA-7s and AA-8s.

THE FRENCH MIRAGE

One final multi-role aircraft which must be mentioned, although really not a single aircraft but a whole family, is the French Dassault-Breguet Mirage. The original Mirage III became famous when it spearheaded the Israeli attack during the Six-day War in 1967 and subsequently became a huge export success. The original sleek delta-wing design has been given enhanced manoeuvrability in the Mirage 5 by the addition of canard foreplanes, as on the Swedish Viggen. The third member of the family, the F1, has basically the same fuselage but conventional wings and tailplanes. The latest Mirage 2000 version bears a superficial resemblance to the original III, reverting to a delta configuration, but in fact is a brand new and far superior machine.

LIGHTWEIGHT FIGHTERS

The major problem with all the aircraft described so far is that their complexity and sophistication make them very expensive to build and maintain. For that reason, in recent years the lightweight fighter has come into fashion, especially for export to countries without lavish defence budgets.

By far the most important aircraft in this classification is the General Dynamics F-16 Fighting Falcon. Originally built purely as a technology demonstrator, it has won widespread acclaim and been exported to many

ABOVE RIGHT Flight of five F-16 Fighting Falcons armed with wingtip Sidewinder air-to-air missiles. Today this aircraft is one of the most capable in the world and its export success story is sure to continue.

TOP The twin-seat trainer version of the Mirage F1 is just as combat-capable as the single-seat fighter, like most modern high-performance trainers, and is seen here with Super 530 and Magic AAMs.

LEFT Mirage multi-role fighter armed with two Super 530 AAMs, eight 250kg bombs and two drop tanks.

AIR SUPERIORITY AND MULTI-ROLE FIGHTERS

Aircraft name	DIMENSIONS (M)			Loaded weight (kg)	Engine(s)	Max speed (km/h)	Max range (km)	Max ceiling (m)	Main weapons carried
	Length	Height	Span						
Dassault-Breguet Mirage IIIC	14.75	4.25	8.22	8,936	1 × SNECMA 6,000kg turbojet	1,390	1,600	17,000	2 × 30mm, 1,326kg bombs, rockets, etc
Mirage IIIE	15.03	4.25	8.22	13,500	1 × SNECMA 6,200kg turbojet	1,390	1,600	17,000	2 × 30mm, 4,200kg bombs rockets, etc
Mirage 5	15.55	4.25	8.22	13,500	1 × SNECMA 6,200 or 7,200kg turbojet	1,390	1,600	17,000	2 × 30mm, 4,200kg bombs, rockets, etc
McDonnell Douglas F-15 Eagle	19.43	5.63	13.05	25,401	2 × P&W 10,855kg turbofans	2,655	5,560	19,200	AIM-7, AIM-9, AMRAAM, ASRAAM
MiG-23/27 Flogger	16.8	4.35	8.17 to 14.25	19,600	1 × Tumansky turbofan, 12,500kg (MiG-23); 11,500kg (MiG-27)	2,500	1,300 (MiG-23); 2,500 (MiG-27)	18,600 (MiG-23); 15,500 (MiG-27)	1 × 23mm,,AA-7 AA-8 (MiG-23); AS-7, AS-10 (MiG-27)
MiG-25 Foxbat	23.82	6.1	13.95	36,200	2 × Tumansky 11,250kg turbojets	3,400	1,450 (combat radius)	24,400	AA-6, AA-7, AA-8
MiG-29 Fulcrum	15.5	4.9	12.0	16,700	2 × 7,500kg turbofans	2,450	670 (combat radius)	?	AA-10
MiG-31 Foxhound	25.57	6.1	14.0	41,000	2 × 14,000kg turbofans	2,550	1,500 (combat radius)	23,000	AA-9
Panavia Tornado F3 ADV	18.06	5.7	8.6 to 13.9	21,546 (on take-off)	2 × Turbo-Union 7,258kg + turbofans	2,414	600+ (combat radius)	?	1 × 27mm, Sky Flash, ASRAAM, AIM-9, AMRAAM
Sukhoi Su-27 Flanker	20.5	6.0	14.0	35,000	2 × 12,700kg turbofans	2,500	1,150 (combat radius)	13,000+	AA-10

BELOW F-16 dropping a load of free-fall bombs, displaying the aircraft's dual-role capability.

countries as well as being built in large numbers for the USAF. The Soviet Su-27 was specifically developed to meet the threat posed by the nimble F-16, which is probably the greatest tribute to its capabilities.

Bald figures say nothing about the F-16's exceptional manoeuvrability, its ability to pull 9g in sustained turns with a full weapons load, its small radar signature, the pilot's superb visibility or its amazing load-carrying capability considering its size. It is armed with an M61 Vulcan and normally carries a Sidewinder on each wingtip, while its under-fuselage pylon can carry either a 1,136-litre (300-US gallon) drop tank or a 1,000kg (2,200lb) bomb. Wing pylons can carry an additional 7,892kg (17,400lb) of any bombs or missiles in the enormous US inventory, so the F-16 is capable of delivering a massive strike and defending itself in a dog-fight on the way in if necessary.

Other lightweight fighter/attack aircraft include the Italian Aermacchi MB.339, British Aerospace Hawk, Spanish CASA C-101 Aviojet, Franco-German Dassault Breguet/ Dornier Alpha Jet, Indian HAL Ajeet (based on the British Gnat), and American Northrop F-5. Leading particulars are given in the accompanying table.

V/STOL AND STOVL AIRCRAFT

As noted earlier, aircraft which depend on runways would be hideously vulnerable during a major war. The only aircraft that is completely free of such dependence, the British Aerospace Harrier began life as the P.1127, a research aircraft built with substantial American funding to explore the possibilities of vectored-thrust flight. Thrust vectoring involves swiveling the jet efflux nozzles to direct the aircraft upward, forward or even backward in flight. Even today,

the Harrier is the only operational aircraft which can achieve this, the Soviet Yak-38 forger employing separate nozzles for lift and forward propulsion, even though the latter can be swivelled.

Although this system makes the Harrier tricky and sometimes positively hazardous to fly, it also gives it enormous dogfight manoeuvrability as was proved so conclusively in the Falklands. The main penalty of using the vectored thrust system was that it made early

BELOW BAe Sea Harrier with Sidewinders and drop tanks under its wings.

versions extremely thirsty for fuel, which reduced endurance and load-carrying ability: a major drawback with the GR.1 which first flew in 1967 and with the later GR.3, which became the AV-8A in US Marine Corps service. Subsequently, a joint development programme between British Aerospace and McDonnell Douglas has resulted in the Harrier II – designated GR.5 in RAF service and AV-8B by the US Marines – which has markedly superior performance. The Harrier II has bigger wings for increased lift in level flight, and consequently improved endurance and load-carrying ability. Extensive use has also been made of carbon fibre to reduce weight, while the engine intakes have been enlarged to increase the volume of air and so improve engine efficiency. By early 1988 no plans had been announced to similarly update the Royal Navy's Sea Harriers, though these aircraft will be substantially modified to the new FRS.2 standard in the light of the Falklands' experience. The Sea Harrier is basically a GR.3 with the nose and cockpit revised to accommodate Blue Fox radar.

The Harrier GR.5 is still a small aircraft despite its enlarged wing, but its endurance has been doubled, from one and a half to three hours on combat air patrol 185km (115 miles) from its base, which could be a clearing in the middle of a forest. Weapons load on one under-fuselage and six wing hardpoints can include drop tanks, ECM pods (the Harrier has no integral ECM gear), Sidewinder AAMs, Maverick anti-tank missiles, JP233 airfield attack dispensers and 30mm Aden gun packs. In addition, the basic aircraft has two built-in Adens for dogfighting.

The Sea Harrier is slightly different in configuration, and the new Blue Vixen radar scheduled to replace the Blue Fox of the FRS.1 will give the aircraft a look-down/shoot-down capability over land or sea. Basic weapons fit of the naval Harrier is the same as that of the RAF version but with the addition of the Sea Eagle anti-shipping missile.

By comparison with the Harrier, the Soviet Yak-38 appears fairly crude, even though many aspects of the Anglo-American aircraft's design have obviously been copied. The main difference between the two machine seems to be that while the Harrier is a dual-role aircraft, the Forger is an interceptor designed to take out Western maritime AEW and ASW aircraft. It is larger than the Harrier GR.5 and at one time it was thought to be supersonic, but this theory has now been abandoned.

The Forger is purely a naval aircraft, no ground-based versions being known to exist, and its principal armament is four AA-8 Aphid AAMs or GSh-23 gun pods carried beneath the wings. Like the Harrier, it is a single-seater, though tandem-seat trainers also exist. Current performance estimates are being raised.

ANTI-TANK AIRCRAFT

There are many other military aircraft in service around the world, including dozens of obsolete or obsolescent types, counter-insurgency machines, light trainer/attack aircraft and so on, but only two dedicated anti-tank machines, the US Air Force's Fairchild Republic A-10 Thunderbolt II and the Soviet Sukhoi Su-25 Frogfoot.

The A-10 was conceived as a strictly subsonic strike aircraft with substantial weapons-carrying ability and low infra-red signature to help protect it from infantry-launched surface-to-air missiles. It is also incredibly robust, being capable of staying in the air with half a

wing or an engine missing, while the pilot is himself encased in what has been colloquially described as a bathtub of solid titanium to protect him from ground fire. The A-10 is designed to operate slow and low against enemy tanks, and in addition to a formidable 30mm Gatling-style cannon in its nose it has 11 hardpoints on which can be slung a wide variety of ordnance. Three of these will normally be used for two Sidewinders plus an ECM pod, while the others carry Maverick anti-tank missiles.

The Soviet Union rushed its fences in designing the Su-25, because it is closely based upon the American design which was in competition with the A-10 and lost, the A-9. One

ABOVE Harrier GR 5 under construction. The use of carbon fibre in the wings has helped to greatly improve the aircraft's endurance and load-carrying ability.

RIGHT Harrier GR 3 firing a salvo of 68mm (2¾in) SNEB free-flight rockets. The pointed nose contains the laser target designator. The appendage on the tail is a rear warning radar to detect enemy aircraft approaching from behind.

of the penalties the Western powers have to pay for democracy is relatively free access to information and the Soviet Union has taken advantage of this over the years, as seen elsewhere. In putting the Frogfoot into production the Russians ended up with an aircraft far less capable than the Thunderbolt, one which has proved very vulnerable to the Stinger surface-to-air missiles supplied to the Afghanistan resistance forces by the CIA.

The Su-25 is a high-wing aircraft with long semi-swept wings to enhance loiter time over the battlefield, but its twin engines are mounted low in the fuselage, a fundamental mistake in a weapons platform intended to fly slowly and at minimum altitude in a hostile environment. It forms a smaller target than the A-10 but has a much greater infra-red signature. It is not believed to have a Gatling-style gun but may have a twin-barrel 30mm weapon. Main armament otherwise includes the AS-8 anti-tank missile, unguided rockets, laser-guided bombs and cluster weapons as well as chemical and fire bombs.

LIGHTWEIGHT FIGHTER/ATTACK AIRCRAFT

Aircraft name	DIMENSIONS (M)			Loaded weight (kg)	Engine(s)	Max speed (km/h)	Max range (km)	Main weapons carried
	Length	Height	Span					
Aermacchi MB339	10.97	3.99	10.86	6,150	1 × RR 1,814 or 2,019kg turbojet	907	371 (combat radius)	1,814kg inc Magic, Sidewinder, DEFA 30mm gun pods
BAe Hawk	11.95	4.09	9.4	7,375	1 × RR/Adour 2,586kg turbofan	1,014	1,270	3,085kg inc 30mm centreline gun pod, 2 × Sidewinder
CASA C-101 Aviojet	12.5	4.25	10.6	5,600	1 × Garrett 1,950kg turbofan	797	380 (combat radius)	2,250kg inc 30mm gun pod and 4 × 250kg bombs
Dassault Breguet/Dornier Alpha Jet	12.29	4.2	9.11	7,500	2 × Larzac 1,440kg turbofans	927	2,940 (ferry range)	2,500kg inc 27 or 30mm gun pod, 4 × bombs, ECM pods, etc
General Dynamics F-16 Fighting Falcon	14.52	5.0	9.45	16,057	1 × P&W 10,814kg turbofan	2,173	547 (combat radius)	1 × M61 Vulcan AIM-9 plus 8,892kg stores
HAL Ajeet	9.04	2.69	6.73	4,030	1 × RR 2,118kg turbojet	1,150	1,180	2 × 30mm guns, 2-4 250kg bombs
Northrop F-5E Tiger	14.68	4.06	8.13 excl wingtip AAMs	12,000	2 × GE 2,270kg turbojets	1,734	1,779	3,175kg bombs, rockets, pods, etc plus 2 × 20mm guns and 2 × Sidewinder

ABOVE Fairchild Republic A-10A Thunderbolt II armed with Maverick air-to-surface and anti-tank missiles.

RIGHT The A-10 looks as solid in flight as it is in fact. The engine positions are specially designed to reduce its infra-red signature to ground-launched missiles, and the A-10 has many other 'survivability' features.

RIGHT An Apache firing its chain gun from its swivelling mounting below the fuselage. Although effective weapons, helicopters have proved themselves to be very vulnerable to modern infantry-portable SAMs, as the Russians have discovered to their cost in Afghanistan.

ABOVE The sheer size of the 30mm GAU-8/A Gatling-style gun carried by the A-10 can be appreciated from this view alongside a Volkswagen 'Beetle'.

COMBAT HELICOPTERS

A relative newcomer to the battlefront, since it is really only in the post-1945 era that the helicopter has become sufficiently reliable and sophisticated to be of fighting value, these aircraft today fulfill a wide range of roles, the most important being anti-tank and anti-submarine. There are far too many combat helicopters in existence to analyze in detail so the following are taken as representative, although brief data on other major types are included in the table.

The most impressive – and expensive – machine is the American McDonnell Douglas AH-64 Apache. Intended to supplement and eventually replace the Bell HueyCobra, which earned a considerable reputation in Vietnam as a gunship, the Apache is fast, heavily armed wth a 30mm cannon and up to 16 Hellfire missiles, and like the A-10, heavily armoured to enable it to survive in the low-level attack role. It can operate by night as well as by day thanks to its new infra-red night vision system, which is coupled to displays presented in the visors of the crew's helmets. The Apache also has laser target marking, tracking and ranging equipment and can be flown and operated by the co-pilot (who sits in the front of the cockpit) if the pilot is wounded or killed. Over the battlefield the Apache would operate down on the deck, and in combat it is normal for two or, more usually, three attack helicopters to operate together, for mutual support.

The Apache's 30mm Chain Gun is a single-barrel weapon, its name deriving from the fact that its unlinked rounds are fed on an endless conveyor belt which occupies half the helicopter's interior. It does not have a particularly high rate of fire, only 625rds/min, nor a high muzzle velocity, because American combat experience in Vietnam and elsewhere has shown that neither is necessary against ground targets. In fact, a very high rate of fire is actually wasteful and causes excessive barrel wear, which is compounded by a high muzzle velocity; it is only against aircraft and missiles that they are needed. The Apache's gun is positioned on a swivelling mount beneath the forward fuselage and is driven by an auxiliary electric motor. In addition to American M789/799 rounds it can also fire British Aden or French DEFA 30mm rounds, which could be very useful in a European war environment.

Hellfire, which represents the state of the art in air-launched anti-tank missiles, is a fire-and-forget missile which homes either on a target marked by the Apache's own laser or one marked by another helicopter, fixed-wing aircraft or ground-based designator. This facility enables the attacking helicopter to hide behind a fold in the ground or a ridge and launch its

ABOVE The effect of a Hellfire missile hitting a Soviet T-62 tank!

RIGHT the Hughes AH-64 Apache is the most formidable combat helicopter in the world with its combination of 30mm chain gun and Hellfire missiles.

OPPOSITE The Bell AH-1 HueyCobra is probably the best-known combat helicopter series in the world as a result of its extensive use in Vietnam, and a continuous programme of modernization will keep it in service up to the turn of the century. This is an AH-1W SuperCobra.

missiles without being spotted by enemy anti-aircraft defences. Hellfire is a solid-fuel missile which burns without emitting a trail of smoke to give away its presence. It is supersonic and while its range is classified it is said by the US Department of Defense to be far in excess of present anti-armour systems. The warhead is a large shaped charge 178mm (7in) in diameter and weighing 9kg (20lb) which can only be defeated by a combination of Chobham and reactive armour. The Apache can fire all its missiles more or less simultaneously if enough target markers are operative. In due course the A-10 Thunderbolt may also be equipped with the Hellfire.

Soviet equivalent of the Apache is the new Mil Mi-28 Havoc, which is believed to be very similar in configuration. A twin-engined tandem-seat dedicated attack helicopter, whereas earlier Russian designs have all been multi-role, it has a nose gun of approximately 30mm calibre in the same position as the Chain Gun on the American machine and is said to be capable of carrying eight AS-8 (air-launched AT-6) missiles.

The single most important maritime helicopter in the world is the Sikorsky S-61 Sea King, which is in service with many Western and other navies, including those of Australia, Brazil, Egypt, India, Italy, Japan, Pakistan, the UK, the USA and West Germany. A large and

extremely versatile helicopter, it can be operated in almost any mode from troop transport to casualty evacuation, and from air/sea search and rescue (SAR) to airborne early warning platform, but its principal role is the crucial one of anti-submarine warfare. It can carry the most up-to-date radar, dipping sonar and magnetic anomaly detector equipment as well as up to four homing torpedoes or nuclear depth bombs. Although it is being replaced in the US Navy by the Sikorsky SH-60B Seahawk, and despite being nearly 30 years old, it is still of vital significance in NATO.

Details of other current combat helicopters are included in the accompanying table.

ABOVE A submarine's eye view of a Sea King as it lowers its dunking sonar into the ocean.

BELOW A US Navy Sea King anti-submarine helicopter lands aboard a carrier.

COMBAT HELICOPTERS

Helicopter name/type	Country of Origin	Main role(s)	DIMENSIONS (M) Length	Height	Loaded weight (kg)	Max speed (km/h)	Range (km)	Main weapons load
Aérospatiale Gazelle	France	Anti-tank and land and ship-borne utility	9.35	3.18	10.5	1,800	264	755	4-6 HOT[1] or AS.12 or similar AT missiles
Aérospatiale Puma	France	Troop carrier and anti-shipping	14.06	4.92	15.0	7,400	271	572	20mm gun, 2 × Exocet or 2 × torpedoes
Agusta A109A	Italy	Multi-role	10.71	3.3	11.0	2,600	272	556	TOW[2], rocket pods or Otomat[3]
Agusta A129 Mangusta (Mongoose)	Italy	Anti-tank	12.275	3.35	11.9	3,700	270	625	4 × TOW or Hellfire or 4 × 70mm pods each with 52 unguided rockets
Bell OH-58 Kiowa	America	Anti-tank and utility	12.49	2.91	10.77	1,814	188+	555	2-4 × TOW, 2 × Stinger AAM[4]
Bell AH-1 Huey Cobra	America	Anti-tank and close ground support	13.59 to 17.68	4.12	13.41 to 14.63	2,754 to 6,350	277 to 333	574	20 or 30mm Gatling-type gun, 7.62mm Minigun, up to 8 × TOW
Hughes OH-6 Defender	America	Multi-role anti-tank or anti-ship	9.24	2.48	8.03	1,361	241	611	2 × torpedoes, 4 × TOW or 14 × unguided rockets
Kaman SH-2 Seasprite	America	Anti-submarine	12.3	4.14	13.41	6,033	270	679	2 × torpedoes, sonobuoys, etc; 2 × Sparrow or Sidewinder
Kamov Ka-25 Hormone	Russia	Anti-submarine and missile guidance	10.36	5.4	15.75	7,500	209	650	2 × torpedoes or nuclear depth bombs
Kamov Ka-27 Helix	Russia	As Ka-25	11.0	5.5	16.75	11,500	260+	600	As Ka-25
MBB B0105	West Germany	Multi-role	11.86	3.0	9.84	2,622	270	575	6 × TOW or HOT
McDonnell Douglas AH-64 Apache	America	Anti-tank and close ground support	14.68	4.26	14.63	8,006	300	689	1 × 30mm Hughes M230A1 chain gun, Hellfire
Mil Mi-8/-17 Hip	Russia	Ground attack and utility	18.31	5.65	21.29	12,000 (−8) or 13,000 (−17)	260	480	8 × 57mm rocket pods or 2 × AT-2 or AT-3 anti-tank missiles[5]
Mil Mi-24 Hind	Russia	As Mi-8	17.0	4.25	17.0	11,500	320	160	1 × 12.7mm DSHk gun, 4 × 57mm rocket pods or 4 × AS-8 (AT-6) anti-tank missiles
Sikorsky S-61 Sea King	America	Multi-role	16.7	5.1	18.9	9,299	267	1,160	Anti-ship and anti-submarine weapons according to user country
Sikorsky SH-70 Hawk family	America	Multi-role	12.6 to 19.76	5.13 to 5.23	16.36	Up to 9,979	296	805	2 × torpedoes, mines, depth bombs or up to 16 × Hellfire
Westland Lynx	France	Multi-role anti-tank, ship or submarine	15.16 to 15.47	3.66	12.8	4,535 (army) to 4,763 (navy)	322	540	8 × HOT, TOW, AS.12 or Hellfire, 4 × Sea Skua[6] or 2 × torpedoes

[1]HOT – Haut-subsonique Optiquement teleguide Tire d'un tube; French anti-tank missile. See next chapter.
[2]TOW – Tube-launched Optically-tracked Wire-guided anti-tank missile; see next chapter.
[3]Otomat – Franco-Italian turbojet-powered anti-shipping cruise missile. Range circa 100km, warhead 210kg.
[4]American light, anti-aircraft missile – see next chapter.
[5]See next chapter.
[6]British anti-shipping missile with range of 20km and 20kg warhead.

4

FIREPOWER
ON LAND

For centuries the epitome of firepower has been the cannon. To some extent this is still true, but the traditional artillery piece has recently been joined by tanks and missiles. Today the main battle tank (MBT) is the principal symbol of land-based firepower, and the tank is certainly the most flexible, hard-hitting and survivable weapons system in the hands of any army commander.

The modern MBT is a most impressive machine, a far cry from the lumbering monsters which faltered across the barbed wire and trenches of the Western Front in 1917–18 at barely walking pace, or even those which spearheaded Hitler's Blitzkrieg assaults of 1939–41. At first sight a tank appears indestructible, and its squat massiveness, the solidity of its armour plate, the size of its gun and the roar of its engine are intrinsically terrifying.

However, the modern MBT is not just all muscle and no brain: its onboard computer systems, laser rangefinders, night vision apparatus and suchlike are just as sophisticated as anything found in a warship or combat aircraft, and usually much tougher to withstand the continuous jolting and vibration.

The most potent of all modern MBTs are the American M1 and M1A1 Abrams, the British Challenger, the West German Leopard 2, Soviet T–64/–72/–80 and the Israeli Merkava. Details of other current types such as Chieftain, M60 and AMX-30 are given in the accompanying table. Of the foregoing, Challenger is head of the league so will be considered first.

CHALLENGER

Challenger was not originally designed to meet a British requirement, but an upgraded Chieftain with Chobham armour developed for Iran. With the fall of the Shah the British Army benefited, since there was no other customer for the tanks already built or half-built. Challenger's frontal armour is said to be the equivalent of 610mm (24in) of conventional plate while its Condor engine gives it twice the power-to-weight ratio of the Chieftain. Coupled with improved suspension and fire-control apparatus, this makes it both reliable and relatively comfortable over the worst feasible terrain. Moreover, its 120mm (4¾in) rifled gun is the most accurate and powerful in the world. With a high speed and low, well-sloped silhouette, Challenger is also a difficult target.

Challenger's 120mm (4¾in) gun can fire a variety of ammunition, including solid armour-piercing discarding sabot (APDS), high-explosive squash head (HESH) and the new fin-stabilized discarding sabot shaped-charge rounds described in the introduction. This gun, the same as that in the earlier Chieftain, has a muzzle velocity with tungsten-carbide-cored rounds of 1,370m/sec (4,500ft/sec). The laser sighting and computerized fire-control systems give it a 90 per cent chance of a first-round hit at anything up to 3,500m (3,825yd). The tank normally carries 64 rounds of ammunition and a good crew can loose off around ten rounds a minute.

M1 ABRAMS

The M1 has the American-built version of the British 105mm (4⅛in) gun first used so successfully on the old Centurion, but the M1A1 has a 120mm (4¾in) smoothbore gun of Ger-

man design identical to that in the Leopard 2: otherwise the two models are virtually identical. The Abrams is the first new American MBT for years, for the US Army has had to make do with various updates of the obsolescent M60 since the 1960s. Even so, it is still no match for Challenger, since the gun is only stabilized in the horizontal plane. This means it is not as accurate while firing on the move.

Otherwise the Abrams is an excellent design, especially since the British government shared the secret of Chobham armour with the Americans. It has special safety features, such as the ammunition being sealed off from the crew compartment by a strengthened bulkhead

BELOW Testing a self-forging fragment against a target. The explosion squeezes the lens-shaped round into a pointed armour-piercing projectile which is hurled at incredible velocity through the relatively thin upper armour of the tank.

LEFT British Army Challenger main battle tanks during an exercise in Germany recently.

ABOVE The 120mm (4$^{7}/_{10}$in) smoothbore gun fitted to the Leopard 2 is good, without question, but it is doubtful whether in combat it would prove as accurate as the rifled British gun of the same calibre.

FAR LEFT An American M1 Abrams during the same exercise in Germany. The flat plates of Chobham armour on the turret and the well-sloped hull front confer excellent protection and the tank's firepower is only excelled by that of the Challenger and Chieftain.

LEFT From the front, the Leopard 2 has the same slab-sided appearance as the Abrams and Challenger, presenting a turret with almost vertical faces. The tube alongside the barrel is the laser rangefinder.

and contained in a bin at the rear of the turret which will explode upward rather than inward if hit.

Unlike the British tank, which has a diesel engine, the Abrams has a gas turbine which starts more readily in really cold weather such as is often experienced on the north German plain, is very quiet and, being more compact than a petrol or diesel engine of comparable power, can be changed more easily in the field for repair or maintenance. However, it runs very hot, especially when the tank is not moving, giving rise to an infra-red signature which acts as a beacon for infra-red homing missiles.

Although exact figures for armour penetration are classified, it is said that the 120mm (4¾in) smoothbore gun firing fin-stabilized rounds can penetrate the same thickness at 2,200m (2,400yd) as the 105mm (4⅛in) rifled gun firing spin-stabilized projectiles can pierce at 1,800m (1,970yd). Obviously, both are inferior to the 120mm (4¾in) gun on Challenger and Chieftain. The M1 carries 55 rounds of ammunition while the M1A1 has only 40.

LEOPARD 2

The West German Leopard 2 is armed with the same Rheinmetall 120mm (4¾in) smoothbore gun as the M1A1, and it carries 42 rounds. The Germans have produced an excellent all-round vehicle combining good firepower with speed, manoeuvrability and armour protection. The turret and glacis are faced with Chobham armour which confers a slab-sided appearance to the superstructure, but otherwise, like the Challenger and Abrams, the Leopard 2 has well sloped armour plates to help deflect solid armour-piercing rounds and dissipate the effect of shaped-charge projectiles. The Netherlands Army has purchased several hundred Leopard 2s and the Swiss manufacture it under licence for their own armed forces.

Like that on Challenger, its gun is stabilized in both azimuth and elevation which confers great accuracy in conjunction with its integrated laser rangefinder and fire-control system. Passive night vision equipment is similarly standard.

SOVIET MBTs

On the other side of the fence, the latest Soviet tanks are also very capable, and in addition to featuring a form of composite armour similar to the Chobham design have recently been observed covered with tiles of reactive armour copied from Israeli vehicles captured in the Lebanon. Even so, Israeli tanks with the British 105mm (4⅛in) gun have succeeded in knocking out many of the much newer Soviet designs during the fighting there.

Earliest of the modern Russian tanks is the T-64, which began to be replaced by the T-72 after it had only been in production for two years, suggesting that the Red Army finds it unsatisfactory. Both are very similar in external appearance, with well sloped hull armour and the typical flat saucer-shaped turret which has characterized all Soviet tanks since World War II.

The main internal difference between the two designs is that the T-64 is powered by a 750bhp diesel engine and the T-72 by a 780bhp multi-fuel design. External fuel drums can be carried to extend range, though these are discarded when going into action. Armour thickness of the T-72 is up to 203mm (8in) on the glacis. Both are armed with a 125mm (5in) smooth-bore gun firing fin-stabilized ammunition, 40 rounds being carried by the T-64 and 39 by the T-72. The use of an automatic carousel-style loading mechanism has allowed the crew to be reduced to three men compared with four in the Western tanks described above.

Recently a new Soviet MBT has gone into production, designated T-74 by the Soviets but called T-80 by NATO. Although no details are available it is believed this vehicle is powered by a gas turbine engine, like the Abrams.

BELOW Soviet T-72s during an exercise. The low silhouette and saucer-shaped turret are typical of all post-war Russian tanks.

RIGHT A Swingfire missile at the moment of launch from a British Striker, the dedicated anti-tank member of the Scorpion family of light tracked AFVs.

MERKAVA

For years the Israeli Army has persevered with cast-offs from abroad, such as the British Centurion, the American M48 and M60, the little French AMX-13 and even the wartime M4 Sherman. Although the Israelis have constantly upgraded them, improving the engines, transmission, armour protection and fire-control, they have always had to face the problem that foreign governments might at some point cease to supply them. Indeed, at one point they were to have received British Chieftains but the government of the day cancelled the contract after two trials vehicles had been supplied. Following the Six-day War in 1967, therefore,

RIGHT The T-74/-80 is the latest in a long line of progressively upgraded Soviet MBTs and incorporates technology equal to anything in the West although crew comfort has been sacrificed for a small profile. This gives individual vehicles reduced effective endurance, but the Russians have more tanks . . .

Israeli engineers began designing a brand new tank to their own specification, and the resulting Merkava (chariot) began entering service in 1979.

The Merkava is a most unusual tank. It has its 900bhp diesel engine at the front, where it helps protect the crew, and a large compartment at the rear which can house up to ten infantrymen in addition to the crew of four if the ammunition carried is halved (from 92 to 46). Other unusual features include the very small turret containing the same 105mm (4⅛in) gun as on the M1 Abrams, and the fact that the diesel fuel is contained in the hull front, sandwiched between two layers of armour plate. The Israelis have not been given access to the secret of Chobham armour but this system is said to confer considerable extra protection against hollow-charge warheads.

LIGHT ARMOURED FIGHTING VEHICLES

A wide variety of other AFVs are used by modern armies. Ranging from armoured cars and light gun- or missile-armed tracked vehicles to large self-propelled artillery pieces, they are far too numerous for individual consideration, and only representative examples can be described here.

MISSILE CARRIERS

The Soviet Union pioneered the deployment of anti-tank guided weapons on light wheeled and tracked vehicles which have good mobility and offer their crews some protection from small arms fire and nuclear fallout, chemical and biological weapons. The principal example is the BRDM-2 armoured car, which has six launch rails for the AT-5 wire-guided missile

BELOW The commander and gunner of a Scorpion light armoured reconnaissance vehicle peer forward over their 76mm (3in) gun.

or the more recent AT-6 Spiral laser-guided weapon. The former has a 170mm (7in) warhead capable of penetrating around 500mm (20in) of vertical armour plate, which means that only tanks with Chobham armour are immune to it, while the latter has an even larger warhead said to be capable of penetrating 650mm (25½in). Maximum range of the AT-5 is 4,000m (4,375yd), but AT-6 can be guided to its target by a laser designator in another vehicle, aircraft or helicopter, so it can operate out of the launch vehicle's line of sight to a range estimated to be as much as 10,000m (11,000yd).

The BRDM-2 is a four-wheeled vehicle with a crew of four, the launch rails being installed beneath the roof, which is hydraulically raised into its firing position; a total of 14 missiles can be carried internally.

The closest Western equivalent to the BRDM-2 is the British Striker, which also houses its missiles in elevating launchers at the rear of the roof. Striker is one member of the Scorpion family of light tracked AFVs, the other armed versions being Scorpion itself, which has a 76mm (3in) gun firing HESH ammunition, and Scimitar, which has a quick-firing 30mm Rarden cannon. Striker carries the

greatest firepower, in the form of ten Swingfire wire-guided missiles, five in the launch tubes and five in the crew compartment.

Swingfire is a large subsonic missile with a warhead of undisclosed size said to be capable of destroying any known tank. Its operator guides it in flight by means of a miniature joystick to a maximum range of 4,000m (4,375yd).

The third most important vehicle in this class is the West German Marder Milan, which

ABOVE The Milan anti-tank missile launch tube mounted on the 20mm gun turret of the Marder gives this armoured personnel carrier a very capable anti-tank performance.

OPPOSITE BELOW A Scimitar at speed. Its quick-firing 30mm Rarden cannon can inflict enormous damage on light armour and 'soft-skin' vehicles.

OTHER MODERN MAIN BATTLE TANKS

Name/type	Country of Origin	DIMENSIONS (M)			Engine bhp	Max road speed (km/h)	Max road range (km)	Main armament (mm)
		Length	Width	Height				
AMX-30	France	9.48	3.1	2.86	720	65	600	105
Chieftain	Britain	10.79	3.5	2.89	750	48	500	120
Leopard 1	West Germany	9.54	3.37	2.76	830	40	600	105
M60A3	America	9.44	3.63	3.27	750	48	480	105
OF-40	Italy	9.22	3.51	2.68	830	65	600	105
Strv 103 'S tank'	Sweden	8.99	3.63	1.7 to 273[1]	240 and 490[2]	50	390	105
T-62	Russia	9.33	3.3	2.39	580	50	450	115
Type 59	China	9.0	3.27	2.4	580	50	500	100
Type 74	Japan	9.41	3.18	2.22 to 2.67[3]	750	53	300	105
Vijayanta (Vickers MBT Mk 1)	India[4]	9.73	3.17	3.1	800	48	480	105

[1]Although classed as a tank, the Strv 103 is really a self-propelled gun, without a traversing turret. Its most unusual feature is that it can raise or lower itself on its suspension to obtain different angles of elevation and depression, hence the two different heights given.
[2]The Strv's main engine is a 490bhp American-designed gas turbine. As mentioned in the description of the M1 Abrams, these are very good at cold starts (an obvious requirement of the Swedish Army) but give off an enormous amount of heat when the vehicle is stationary. For this reason the Swedes have incorporated an auxiliary 240bhp diesel to keep all systems functional while the tank is stationary, including the hydropneumatic suspension. Other special features of this unusual vehicle are its front-mounted engines and automatic loader for the gun.
[3]Although the Type 74 has a proper turret for its gun, it also employs hydropneumatic suspension. This allows the tank to hide behind a ridge or in a depression in the ground and just 'pop up' to fire.
[4]The Vijayanta is a licence-built version of the Vickers private-venture tank which was specifically designed for export, being simpler and cheaper than Chieftain.

(For full specifications of battle tanks described, see page 126.)

was designed as a troop carrier with a powerful anti-tank capability. To this end it has a small rotating turret containing a 20mm gun and a launcher for the Milan, a standard infantry weapon in most European NATO countries and one which is being fitted to a wide variety of other armoured personnel carriers (APCs).

Milan is a man-portable wire-guided missile with a range of 2,000m (2,190yd). Its warhead is 115mm (4½in) in diameter and is claimed to be able to penetrate armour plate up to a metre thick, which is obviously enough to destroy any enemy AFV. Milan earned a formidable reputation as a bunker-buster when used against Argentinian fortifications in the Falklands.

Finally, the American M2/M3 Bradley, the M2 being a troop carrier and the M3 a reconnaissance variant with increased space inside for stowage of BGM-71 TOW missiles. Each vehicle has two TOW launch tubes on the side of its turrets (which house a 25mm Chain Gun), five and ten reloads being carried respectively. TOW is standard equipment throughout NATO and many other countries. In its latest version, designated TOW-2, it has a warhead 150mm (6in) in diameter containing two compound explosive shaped charges designed to beat the combination of reactive and Chobham-type armour on the latest Soviet tanks.

TOW is wire-guided but unlike Swingfire and similar weapons all the operator has to do is keep the optical sight fixed on the target and a small computer automatically transmits flight correction signals to the missile's control surfaces. It has a range of 3,750m (4,100yd).

ARMOURED CARS

Armoured cars are a rarity these days, the only significant examples still in service being the British Fox, the American Cadillac-Gage Commando and the French AML-90 Eland, which is the principal AFV of the South African Army. All are gun-armed, the American

and French vehicles mounting a 90mm (3½in) weapon capable of firing HEAT ammunition because, although not smoothbores, the pitch of the rifling has been designed to impart minimal spin. Fox has the same 30mm Rarden cannon as Scimitar, and can carry a Milan launcher.

All three are four-wheeled vehicles with crews of three, although there is also a six-wheeled version of the Commando, and while all are used primarily in the reconnaissance role, they have enough firepower to take on relatively lightly armoured vehicles at ranges up to 2,000m (2,190yd).

SELF-PROPELLED ARTILLERY

In many ways, the most important class of AFV is the self-propelled (SP) artillery piece, able to keep up with the tanks and troop carriers and lay down a devastating barrage of high-explosive or nuclear shells, and also able to function as very effective tank-busters.

The main SP artillery weapons are the American 155mm (6¹⁄₁₀in) M109A2, which is also used by the British Army, and the Soviet 152mm (6¹⁄₁₀) 2S3. Both are fully-tracked vehicles with light armoured cabs enclosing the crews and the breech mechanisms of their guns, whereas some other SP guns, such as the 175mm (7in) M107 and 203mm (8in) M110, mount the gun assemblies fully exposed on a tracked hull.

The M109 turret, which is fully traversing through 360 degrees, is mounted at the rear of a modified M113 APC chassis. Its aluminium armour is effective against small arms fire and the whole vehicle is sealed, like almost all modern AFVs, against atmospheric contaminants. Unlike a tank, it cannot fire on the move; instead, it must dig in two hydraulic spades at the rear to absorb the recoil from its large gun. One of its most useful attributes is that it is amphibious, the rotation of its tracks providing propulsion through a lake or river.

The M109 has a crew of six and carries 28 rounds for its 155mm (6¹⁄₁₀in) gun, which incorporates a double muzzle brake to help absorb recoil, as well as a smoke extractor to minimize fumes in the armoured cab or turret. The gun is a very versatile weapon, being able to fire conventional high-explosive shells which are effective against tanks because of their sheer weight. While they will not penet-

ABOVE M109A2 155mm (6¹⁄₁₀in) self-propelled howitzers of the West German Bundeswehr. This is the single most important SPG in the NATO armoury and has a creditable anti-tank capability.

rate the armour of a modern MBT they will demolish all the relatively delicate external equipment, damage wheels and tracks and give the crew concussion. The gun can also fire small nuclear shells, smoke shells or projectiles containing nerve gas.

The Copperhead smart shell is another alternative. This homes on targets illuminated by a laser marker with unerring accuracy, but production was suspended after 2,000 rounds had been manufactured because of their cost, and they are issued solely to the US rapid deployment force. The M109's gun has a range of 18,000–24,000m (19,685–26,245yd), depending on model and ammunition, and is extremely accurate.

The Soviet 2S3 is essentially very similar in design and purpose, with a rear-mounted fully-traversing turret to provide protection for the crew of four. The chassis is fully tracked and armoured and was originally designed as a launch vehicle for surface-to-air missiles, which role it still fulfills. The basic vehicle is lower than the M109, a useful attribute in the direct-fire anti-tank role.

The gun mounted in the 2S3, identical to the Red Army's D20 towed artillery piece, can fire either conventional high-explosive or high-explosive armour-piercing rounds, or a 2kT nuclear projectile; range is 24,000m to 37,000m (26,245–40,465yd), depending on whether they are rocket-assisted.

A similar weapon on a different chassis – that of the PT-76 light tank – is the 2S1 122mm (4⅘in) SP gun, which mounts the amazing

D-30 gun (see below) in a similar lightly armoured turret. Although it lacks a nuclear capability, the gun is even more effective in the anti-tank role than the larger 155mm (6¹/₁₀in) D-20.

Various other countries have attempted to build vehicles equal to the M109/2S3; examples include the Italian Palmaria, Anglo-German SP-70 and French AMX-GCT. The first and last are now in production, but the SP-70, based on the highly successful FH-70 gun/

howitzer, was abandoned in 1987.

ROCKET ARTILLERY

Artillery also includes rockets – unguided freeflight missiles designed to lay down a massive barrage at a selected point and time. This type of weapon is one which was pioneered by the Soviets, who persist in mounting their launchers on unarmoured trucks, despite the fact that the rest of their front-line gear has at least light armour.

BELOW LEFT If and when the SP70 ever gets into service, one of its attributes will be an automatic reloading chute, allowing it to be replenished from outside without exposing its crew to air poisoned by radioactivity, nerve gas or bacteriological agents.

LEFT The Multiple Launch Rocket System (MLRS) can deliver devastating ripple salvoes of 227mm rockets with a variety of different warheads, though none of them at present nuclear.

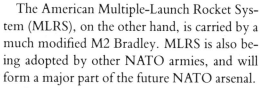

The American Multiple-Launch Rocket System (MLRS), on the other hand, is carried by a much modified M2 Bradley. MLRS is also being adopted by other NATO armies, and will form a major part of the future NATO arsenal.

The MLRS vehicle comprises a fully tracked chassis with an armoured cab at the front housing the crew of three or four men. The rear is taken up with the box-like container for the 12 272kg (600lb) free-flight rockets, which are of 227mm (9in) calibre, have a range of 30km (19 miles) and can be fired singly or in ripple salvos. Like all such systems, MLRS is an area denial weapon: in other words, it lays down a barrage through which enemy troops cannot pass.

In due course the rockets will be fitted with the new Sense And Destroy Armour (SADARM) warhead containing six Skeet self-forging fragments to attack tanks from overhead. At present, however, the main warhead used contains 644 anti-personnel bomblets. Each MLRS vehicle is accompanied in the field by two cargo carriers containing reload rounds.

SP ANTI-AIRCRAFT SYSTEMS

A further important category of armoured fighting vehicles is the self-propelled anti-aircraft gun or missile carrier. There are several of these, the most important being the Soviet ZSU-23-4, SA-4 Ganef, SA-6 Gainful and SA-8 Gecko, the West German Gepard, the French Roland and the British Tracked Rapier. Other air-defence systems are either man-portable or mounted on unarmoured vehicles, the only exception being Shahine, developed in France for Saudi Arabia, which uses the AMX-30 tank chassis as a carrier for six Crotale missiles.

The ZSU-23-4 is a large, fully tracked AFV with a massive turret containing four ZU-23 23mm guns and their associated radar guidance system. The turret is fully rotating to give all-round defence and the liquid-cooled guns have a high rate of fire of 800–1,000rds/min fired in 200-round bursts (50 rounds per barrel). They can elevate to +80 degrees or if necessary can be depressed by as much as −7 degrees, allowing ground targets to be engaged.

The ZSU-23-4 is allocated in very large quantities to each armoured and motorized division in the Red Army and is a formidable low-level air defence system. The Americans spent a great deal of time and money developing a similar weapon system called Sgt York, but ultimately abandoned it.

The SA-4 is a large, long-range surface-to-air missile which is carried in pairs on a fully tracked, lightly armoured vehicle. The missile is launched by four booster rockets which drop away when its sustained-flight ramjet takes over. It has a large warhead and is effective out to 75km (47 miles).

SA-6 is a smaller long-range missile. Three are carried on a similar fully-tracked chassis, which is based on that of the PT-76 light amphibious tank, the guidance radar being carried on a second vehicle. It has a range of up to 60km (37 miles) and an 80kg (176lb) warhead with impact, proximity and infra-red fuzing, and during the 1973 Middle East War Syrian batteries gave the Israeli air force a great deal of trouble.

The SA-8 Gecko is a single-stage, solid-fuel Mach 2 surface-to-air missile with a range of 12km (7½ miles). Six such missiles together

ABOVE MLRS (Multiple Launch Rocket System) developed in the US and deployed by NATO. The basic system consists of a 25-ton tracked vehicle and 12 surface-to-surface free rockets with a range in excess of 30km (18½ miles).

RIGHT Line-up of Soviet ZSU-23-4 self-propelled anti-aircraft guns.

with their target acquisition and guidance radar are carried on the lightly armoured chassis of a six-wheeled amphibious, air-portable truck. The missiles have terminal infra-red guidance, proximity fuzing and fragmentation warheads.

Other, smaller man-portable SAMs can also be carried on armoured personnel carriers. All these weapons are also allocated in large quantities to the armoured and motorized divisions.

The German Gepard is a formidable air-defence weapon comprising two Oerlikon 35mm cannon plus search and tracking radars in a bulky turret on the hull and chassis of a Leopard 1 tank. The vehicle has a crew of three and the guns, which can fire armour-piercing as well as fragmentation rounds, have a rate of fire of 550rds/min.

Roland is a French missile mounted in pairs on each side of an armoured turret on the hull and chassis of the AMX-30 with the acquisition/guidance radar in the middle. The Germans have also adopted this system on their Marder armoured personnel carrier chassis.

Roland can be fired and tracked optically or automatically through the radar; it has a two-stage solid-fuel motor which gives it a speed of Mach 1.6 and a range of 6.3km (4 miles), maximum altitude being 5,000m (16,400ft). It has a high-explosive warhead with impact and proximity fuzes.

The British Rapier is widely acknowledged to be the best short-range ground-based anti-aircraft missile in the world and has been very widely exported; however, so far only the British Army has ordered Tracked Rapier, which is based on the chassis of the American M548 armoured fully tracked cargo carrier. Tracked Rapier has a small armoured cab at the front and a launcher for eight missiles complete with their search and tracking radar at the rear.

Rapier itself is a small missile which is fired at Mach 2+ to a range of 6.5km (4 miles) and maximum altitude of 3,000m (9,850ft), being designed specifically to deal with high subsonic low-flying strike aircraft and cruise missiles. Its extreme accuracy was proved in the Falklands,

ABOVE A Rapier surface-to-air missile is launched from its armoured carrier vehicle which gives an already extremely effective and versatile weapon even greater tactical flexibility.

and it has an impact fuze and semi-armour-piercing high-explosive warhead.

OTHER GROUND WEAPONS

There are so many other weapons that only a selection of the most important can be covered. Conventional towed artillery is still highly significant, the principal gun/howitzers now in service being the Soviet 122mm (4⅘in) D-30 mentioned earlier; the 155mm (6¹⁄₁₀in) FH-70, which is a joint project between Britain, West Germany and Italy; the American 155mm (6¹⁄₁₀in) M198; and the French 155mm (6¹⁄₁₀in) TR.

The Soviet D-30 is mounted on an unusual

carriage copied from a World War II German design. In action it sits on a three-legged platform, the wheels being raised off the ground, which gives it a low profile and the ability to traverse rapidly to any point of the compass – an invaluable asset in anti-tank warfare. For towing (by a lug on the muzzle of the barrel), the legs fold up under the barrel. Its ammunition can include fin-stabilized HEAT, high-explosive fragmentation and chemical rounds fired to long range.

The other three guns, all of which were developed independently to the same basic specification, all have conventional split-trail carriages. Both the FH-70 and TR have small

LEFT Any gun is only a delivery platform, of course. What damages the enemy is the ammunition. Here British gunners fuze high explosive rounds for the 155mm (6¹/₁₀in) FH 70 gun/howitzer.

FIREPOWER ON LAND

OTHER ARMOURED FIGHTING VEHICLES

Name of weapons system	Type of weapon	Country of origin	Length	Width	Height	Engine (bhp)	Road speed (km/h)	Range (km)	Main armament	Specifications
Abbott	105mm SPG/H	Britain	5.84	2.64	5.71	240	48	390	105mm manual	Crew 4. Gun range 17.2km. Too light to do much damage to modern AFVs.
AMX-GCT	155mm SPG/H	France	10.2	3.15	3.3	720	60	450	155mm with auto-load	Fully-revolving turret on AMX-30 chassis. Gun range 24-31, 5km. Crew 4.
AMX-10RC	Recce vehicle	France	9.15	2.95	2.68	260	85	800	105mm in rotating turret	Six-wheeled heavy armoured car only built in small numbers.
ASV-85	85mm tank destroyer	Russia	8.49	2.8	2.1	280	45	260	85mm A/T gun	Used by USSR airborne troops. Crew 4. Almost obsolescent.
BMP-1/2	Infantry combat vehicle	Russia	6.75	2.97	1.98	280	55	500	73mm smoothbore & 2 × AT-3/5/6	Versatile 3 crew + 8 infantry MICV with A/T capability. Amphibious.
Ikv 91	90mm tank destroyer	Sweden	8.845	3.0	2.355	350	69	550	90mm smoothbore	Fully amphibious. Rotating turret. Laser rangefinder.
Jagdpanzer Kanone	90mm tank destroyer	West Germany	8.75	2.98	2.085	500	70	400	90mm rifled gun	Same chassis as Marder. Crew 4. Last of the conventional tankbusters.
M107	175mm SPG	America	11.25	3.15	3.68	405	56	725	175mm 'long rifle' L/60	Long-range (32.7m) Corps support gun also used by UK. Crew 8. No turret.
M110	203mm SPH	America	10.7	3.15	2.93	405	56	725	203mm nuclear cannon	Uses same chassis as M107. Also used by UK. Crew 13. Range 21.3km. No turret.
Palmaria	155mm SPG/H	Italy	11.474	2.35	2.874	750	60	400	155mm with auto-load	Fully-revolving turret on OF-40 chassis. Gun range 24-30km. Crew 5.
PT-76	Light amphibious tank	Russia	7.625	3.18	2.26	240	44	250	76mm	Obsolescent. Crew 3. Used as basis for ZSU-23-4 and other vehicles.
Scorpion/ Scimitar	Recce vehicles	Britain	4.79/ 4.99	2.235/ 2.242	2.102/ 2.096	190	80.5	644	76mm/30mm Rarden	Miniature tanks. Crew 3.
Warrior	Infantry combat vehicle	Britain	5.42	2.8	2.82	800	75	500	30mm Rarden plus 7.62mm Chain Gun	Carries 8 infantry plus 2 crew.

(For full specifications of armoured fighting vehicles described, see page 126.)

117

wheels fitted to the end of the trails and a small auxiliary power unit at the front of the carriage, which allows them to be driven short distances, all being too heavy to be man-handled easily. The FH-70 has a crew of eight and can fire standard HE rounds to 24km (15 miles) or rocket-assisted ammunition to 30km (19 miles).

The French TR has the same crew and identical performance except that its maximum range with rocket-assisted projectiles is 33km (20½ miles). The American M198 is slightly inferior, requiring a crew of ten men and only having a range of 22km (13⅔ miles), or 30km (19 miles) with rocket assistance. FH-70 can traverse through 56 degrees, TR through 65 degrees and M198 through 45 degrees. FH-70 and M198 can both fire the same ammunition, which will eventually include the Copperhead smart anti-tank shell, and all three have muzzle velocities of approximately 830m/sec (2,720ft/sec), depending on ammunition.

MAN-PORTABLE MISSILES

One of the most significant of all postwar developments has been the light man-portable anti-tank and anti-aircraft missile. In the former class we have already seen how effective Milan is: the Soviet equivalent, the AT-4 Spigot, is a line-of-sight wire-guided missile with a range of 2,500m (2,735yd). Control is semi-automatic, the operator having only to keep the target in his sights. The missile has a smaller shaped-charge warhead than Milan, so it will be less effective, particularly against Chobham armour.

The American equivalent, to supplement the vehicle- or helicopter-mounted TOW, is Dragon, a comparatively small missile with a 114mm (4½in) warhead. Guidance is infra-red, and the missile only has a range of 1,000m (1,094yd) so work is proceeding on a replacement. Even lighter anti-armour weapons include the British LAW 80 and the Soviet RPG-18, bazooka-like weapons with ranges of 500m (545yd) and 350m (380yd) respectively, and the Soviet RPG-7, which is basically a hollow-charge grenade launcher with a range of 300m (325yd). The last is one of the most common weapons in the world, having been supplied to many guerilla forces.

In the field of lightweight air defence the most significant weapons are the British Blowpipe/Javelin, the Soviet SA-7 Grail and the American Stinger, which has given Soviet helicopters a hard time in Afghanistan. Blowpipe, which in the improved form called Javelin has a more powerful motor to reduce time to target and extend range to 6km (3¾ miles), is fired at a high supersonic speed from a launch tube over the operator's shoulder. Blowpipe,

RIGHT Although classified as 'man-portable' and using as many lightweight materials in its construction as possible, Milan needs a crew of two and, as can be seen, is very bulky. It is undoubtedly lethal, however!

with a two-stage solid rocket motor which gives it a range of 5km (3 miles), is guided by line-of-sight radio command from the operator's binocular sights and has a proximity-fuzed high-explosive warhead. The system is in service with at least 14 armed forces around the world.

The SA-7 has its own internal infra-red homing head. All the operator has to do is spot the target through his sight and press a button, whereupon the missile automatically locks on ready to be fired. This system is likely to be less effective than Blowpipe because most aircraft today carry flare dispensers, the flares briefly giving out more heat than the aircraft's jet pipe and thereby side-tracking a pursuing missile. The SA-7 missile is a two-stage solid-fuel weapon with a range of 10km (6 miles) and a fragmentation warhead.

The American Stinger is a smaller and lighter system but extremely effective for all that. It uses infra-red guidance like the SA-7, an important difference being that the missile has inbuilt IFF (identification friend or foe) to prevent it accidentally locking onto a friendly aircraft. It is a high-speed – Mach 2 – weapon with a fragmentation warhead and range of 5km (3 miles).

ABOVE An American M198 gun/howitzer in action. Although powerful, the lack of crew protection makes such weapons increasingly vulnerable, hence the tendency towards armoured self-propelled weapons in most modern armies.

5

FIREPOWER IN SPACE

Ever since that historic day of October 4 1957 when Sputnik 1 first started bleeping from orbit it was inevitable that space would become a new battleground. It is axiomatic in warfare that he who holds the high ground has the advantage, both because he can see the enemy dispositions more clearly than the enemy can see his, and because the enemy has to come uphill to get to grips. Another military axiom is that reconnaissance is never wasted, so it is not surprising that only three years after Sputnik America succeeded in launching its first reconnaissance satellite, followed by the Soviet Union two years later. Since then the number and variety of military satellites have increased enormously, with Britain, France and China adding their efforts to those of the superpowers. Russia launches around a hundred military satellites a year, America 'only' twenty, and at any given time there are about 120 functioning in different orbits. The reason that the heavens are not more cluttered is because satellites in low orbits decay and burn up in the atmosphere, so there is a constant erosion of numbers.

The majority of military satellites are 'passive', i.e., concerned with intelligence gathering and mapping, with communications and navigation and with meteorology. Some also serve as long-range early warning instruments, their sensitive detectors probing the electromagnetic spectrum to detect the faint emissions from enemy sites which show that a missile is being readied for firing. All are vital to NATO and the Warsaw Pact, for air, ground and sea forces are almost totally reliant upon satellite communications. In recent years, therefore, considerable effort has been devoted to finding ways of destroying the enemy's satellites. America planned an anti-satellite missile launched from F-15s, with two squadrons operational at Langley and McChord AFBs, but this was cancelled. As early as 1968 the Soviet Union successfully launched two satellites in its Cosmos series, one of which destroyed the other, and today there are a hundred ABM-1B Galosh missiles with an anti-satellite capability deployed in four sites around Moscow. Although these large three-stage missiles, with a range in excess of 320km (200 miles) and 2–3MT warheads, are principally intended as anti-ballistic missile defences designed to knock out incoming ICBMs at the fringe of the atmosphere, they could certainly reach the lower orbital altitudes primarily used by reconnaissance satellites. However, navigation satellites travel higher, communications satellites higher still, and early warning ones highest of all; Galosh could not reach these.

To achieve these higher orbits the Soviet Union uses the SS-9 missile to launch a 2,000kg (4,400lb) high-explosive fragmentation warhead into space on a trajectory which will allow it to catch up with its target within a couple of orbits. The warhead incorporates small thrusters to allow it to manoeuvre and some form of proximity fuzing which ex-

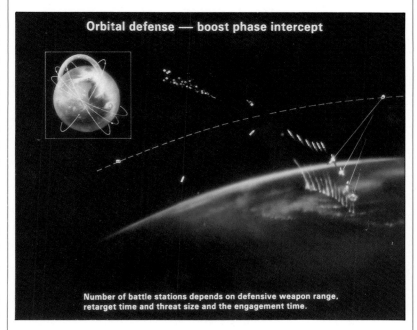

Orbital defense — boost phase intercept

Number of battle stations depends on defensive weapon range, retarget time and threat size and the engagement time.

LEFT An electromagnetic launcher developed by the SDI Organization's Innovative Science and Technology office; an EML can accelerate projectiles to ultra-high velocities using electrical and magnetic energy. Its intended role in strategic defence would be to launch projectiles against ballistic missiles or re-entry vehicles.

OPPOSITE Another idea being explored is the use of electromagnetic guns which accelerate anti-missile or anti-satellite projectiles by means of magnetic accelerator coils rather than using an explosive propellant. Such systems have been laboratory-tested but could only work properly in the vacuum of space.

ABOVE Artist's impression of a Soviet anti-satellite interceptor.

RIGHT A space-based laser system would allow the interception of ballistic missiles in the boost phase, before they can deploy their warheads and decoys. The laser could also theoretically penetrate the atmosphere, and thus be deployed against air-breathing missiles or even aircraft.

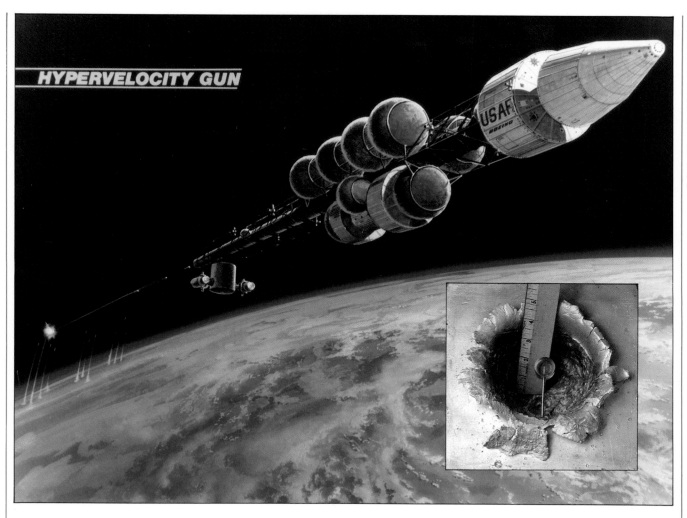

HYPERVELOCITY GUN

plodes it at about a kilometre (1,100yd) from its target. It throws out a shower of metal fragments at high velocity which destroys or certainly incapacitates the enemy satellite. However, because it is only to be expected that the SS-9 launch would be detected and that in many cases the opposing satellite would incorporate its own manoeuvring thrusters to evade the pursuit, the Russians have pioneered a new technique known as grazing, using the same SS-9 missile and a modified warhead. This is launched into a lower orbit than the target satellite which enables it to catch up with it much more quickly. Then, at the appropriate moment, a booster rocket hurls the anti-satellite warhead upwards towards its target, giving it less time to manoeuvre out of danger.

THE LASER KILLERSAT

Two other concepts currently being explored are the space mine and the laser killersat. The former would in effect be an orbiting nuclear device which in time of war would be man-

oeuvred towards its target and detonated. It is the killersat which is commanding the most interest. This would be a manoeuvrable satellite placed in a stable orbit from which it could aim its laser to burn out the 'eyes' and 'ears' of enemy satellites. Its main advantage over the space mine is that it would be re-usable, so could knock out more than one enemy satellite. However, it is fairly easy to defend a satellite against a laser by means of light mirrored screens, so it is likely that the next generation of military satellites will incorporate these. Mirrors can also be used in another way, although the problem of accurate control is enormous. A killersat could direct its beam toward a friendly satellite which would have movable mirrors around it. The laser beam could thus be redirected to a target which would otherwise be out of the killersat's direct line of sight. It is also possible that large and very powerful ground-based lasers capable of punching through the atmosphere could be employed in the same way, aimed at orbiting

ABOVE Artist's impression of the deployment of the EML now under development in the US (see page 121). The hypervelocity launcher would employ electrical forces to fire 'smart' weapons at velocities far in excess of anything possible with chemical propellants.

INSET, ABOVE Kinetic Energy Weapons (KEW) test, Santa Barbara, part of the SDI research programme. The Lexan projectile, which weighed just 7 grammes, was fired from a light gas gun at the cast aluminium block at 23,000 feet per second. Could such KE weaponry play a part in a multi-layered defence against ballistic missiles?

ABOVE Artist's impression of a Soviet ground-based laser; such lasers are already capable of interfering with the functioning of Western satellites.

LEFT Free Electron Laser technology; part of an experimental infra-red FEL undergoing tests before installation. FELs offer the potential for developing a short-wavelength ground-based laser weapon that could penetrate the atmosphere.

RIGHT The reality of today's laser weaponry: the US Air Force version of the Tri-service laser device destroys an MQM-33B drone at Kirtland Air Force Base, New Mexico.

ABOVE RIGHT This artist's impression shows the coherent light beam from powerful ground-based lasers being redirected on to their targets by orbital mirror satellites.

mirrors which would redirect their beams to the chosen targets. The Soviet Union is known to have at least three experimental ground-based laser installations operational.

THE X-RAY LASER

Such weapons need not simply be used against each other, they could also be used to destroy, or at least incapacitate the guidance systems of, enemy ICBMs, and in the United States a great deal of work has been done along these lines

since 1983, when President Reagan announced his Strategic Defense Initiative (SDI), popularly known as the 'Star Wars' programme. One device which is apparently arousing a great deal of interest in this field is the X-ray laser. These are immensely powerful and in fact require the power of the atom to fire them. The hypothesis is that a number of X-ray laser rods would be built around an orbital nuclear bomb like the space mine. These could be aimed at a large number of targets, since the laser rods themselves would be very small. When the nuclear bomb was detonated, each rod would emit a brief but intensely strong beam of energy. These would pierce any satellite defences designed to protect against conventional chemical lasers. Its drawback is its massive size.

A simpler anti-missile device being developed in America is the Homing Overlay. This is a relatively lightweight disc propelled by guided missile towards the incoming ICBM. Seconds before contact the disc unfurls, springing out into a number of 2m (6½ft) long steel spokes which improve the projectile's chance of hitting and destroying its target. The device was tested successfully in 1983.

The problem in the development of all such weapons is that whichever side first develops the potential for an operational anti-missile system lays itself open to a pre-emptive strike from the other side before the defence system is deployed. The possibility of pre-emptive action is extremely disturbing.

ARMOURED FIGHTING VEHICLES

Name of weapons system	Type of weapon	Country of origin	DIMENSIONS (M)			Engine (bhp)	Road speed (km/h)	Range (km)	Main Armament	Specifications
			Length	Width	Height					
2S1	122mm SPG	Russia	7.3	2.85	2.4	240	60	500	122mm	Crew 4
2S3	152mm SPG/H	Russia	7.73	3.2	2.72	500	50	300	152mm	Crew 4
AML-90 Eland	Armoured car	France (used by South Africa)	3.79	1.98	2.07	90	100	600	90mm	Crew 3
BRDM-2	ATGW carrier	Russia	5.75	2.35	2.31	140	100	750	AT-5/-6	Crew 4
Commando	Armoured car	America	5.68	2.26	2.43	155	88	950	90mm	Crew 3
Fox	Armoured car	Britain	5.36	2.13	2.2	190	104	430	30mm Rarden	Crew 3
Gepard	SAM carrier	West Garmany	7.7	3.25	4.03	830	40	600	2 × 35mm	Crew 3
M2/M3 Bradley	Infantry combat vehicle	America	6.45	3.2	2.97	300	66	384	TOW + 25mm Chain Gun	Crew 3 + 6 infantry (M2) or 2 infantry (M3)
M109	155mm SPG	America	6.61	3.29	3.06	405	56	390	155mm	Amphibious Crew 6
MLRS	Rocket artillery	America	6.97	2.97	2.59	500	64	483	227mm rockets	Crew 3–4.
Roland	SAM carrier	France	6.65	3.1	3.2	720	65	600	Roland missiles	Crew 3
Striker	ATGW carrier	Britain	4.83	2.24	2.21	190	80	483	Swingfire	Crew 3. Missiles can be guided by remote control
ZSV-23-4	SP AA gun	Russia	6.3	2.95	2.25	240	44	260	4 × 23mm	Crew 4

MAIN BATTLE TANKS

Name/type	Country of Origin	DIMENSIONS (M)			Engine bhp	Max road speed (km/h)	Max road range (km)	Main armament (mm)
		Length	Width	Height				
Challenger	Britain	11.56	3.52	2.95	1,200	60	500+	120
Leopard 2	West Germany	9.67	3.7	2.76	1,500	72	550	120
M1 Abrams	America	9.77	3.65	2.88	1,500	72	475	105
M1A1 Abrams	America	9.83	3.66	2.88	1,500	67	475	120
Merkava	Israel	8.63	3.7	2.75	900	46	400	105
T-64	Russia	9.1	3.38	2.39	750	70	450	125
T-72	Russia	9.24	3.6	2.37	780	60	480	125

CRUISERS

Cruiser Class	Country of Origin	DIMENSIONS (M)			Displacement (tons)	Speed (knots)	Major weapons fit
		Length	Beam	Draught			
Kirov	Russia	248.0	23.0	8.0	28,000	30	20 × SS-N-19, 16 × SS-N-14, 12 × SA-N-6, 2 × 100 or 130mm, 3 × Ka-25
Slava	Russia	187.0	20.0	8.0	12,000	34	SS-N-12, SA-N-6, SA-N-4, SA-N-7, 2 × 130mm
Sovremenny	Russia	155.0	17.0	6.0	7,950	33	SS-N-22, SA-N-7, 4 × 130mm
Ticonderoga	America	171.7	17.0	9.4	9,600	30	SM-1, Harpoon, Tomahawk, ASROC, 2 × 127mm
Udaloy	Russia	162.0	18.0	6.0	8,000	35	SS-N-14, SA-N-8, 2 × 100mm
Virginia	America	178.0	19.0	9.0	11,000	30	ASROC, Harpoon, Tomahawk, 1 × 127mm

INDEX